KU-765-473

JOHN BERRYMAN

Selected Poems
1938–1968

FABER & FABER

First published in 1972
by Faber & Faber Ltd
Bloomsbury House
74–77 Great Russell Street
London WC1B 3DA

First published in this edition in 2014

Typeset by Faber & Faber Ltd
Printed and bound in Italy by L. E. G. O. S.p.A

All rights reserved
© The Estate of John Berryman 1952, 1959, 1962,
1963, 1964, 1965, 1967, 1968, 1972, 1977

The right of John Berryman to be identified as author
of this work has been asserted in accordance with Section 77
of the Copyrights, Designs and Patents Act 1988

*This book is sold subject to the condition that it shall not, by way of trade
or otherwise, be lent, resold, hired out or otherwise circulated without the
publisher's prior consent in any form of binding or cover other than that
in which it is published and without a similar condition including
this condition being imposed on the subsequent purchaser*

A CIP record for this book is available from the British Library

ISBN 978-0-571-32206-0

2 4 6 8 10 9 7 5 3 1

CONTENTS

From The Dispossessed (1948)

From His Thought Made Pockets (1958)

Berryman's Sonnets (1952, 1967)

Homage to Mistress Bradstreet (1953)

from
THE DISPOSSESSED
(1948)

Winter Landscape

The three men coming down the winter hill
In brown, with tall poles and a pack of hounds
At heel, through the arrangement of the trees
Past the five figures at the burning straw,
Returning cold and silent to their town,

Returning to the drifted snow, the rink
Lively with children, to the older men,
The long companions they can never reach,
The blue light, men with ladders, by the church
The sledge and shadow in the twilit street,

Are not aware that in the sandy time
To come, the evil waste of history
Outstretched, they will be seen upon the brow
Of that same hill: when all their company
Will have been irrecoverably lost,

These men, this particular three in brown
Witnessed by birds will keep the scene and say
By their configuration with the trees,
The small bridge, the red houses and the fire,
What place, what time, what morning occasion

Sent them into the wood, a pack of hounds
At heel and the tall poles upon their shoulders,
Thence to return as now we see them and
Ankle-deep in snow down the winter hill
Descend, while three birds watch and the fourth flies.

The Traveller

They pointed me out on the highway, and they said
'That man has a curious way of holding his head.'

They pointed me out on the beach; they said 'That man
Will never become as we are, try as he can.'

They pointed me out at the station, and the guard
Looked at me twice, thrice, thoughtfully & hard.

I took the same train that the others took,
To the same place. Were it not for that look
And those words, we were all of us the same.
I studied merely maps. I tried to name
The effects of motion on the travellers,
I watched the couple I could see, the curse
And blessings of that couple, their destination,
The deception practised on them at the station,
Their courage. When the train stopped and they knew
The end of their journey, I descended too.

The Spinning Heart

The fireflies and the stars our only light,
We rock, watching between the roses night
If we could see the roses. We cannot.
Where do the fireflies go by day, what eat?
What categories shall we use tonight?
The day was an exasperating day,
The day in history must hang its head
For the foul letters many women got,
Appointments missed, men dishevelled and sad
Before their mirrors trying to be proud.
But now (we say) the sweetness of the night
Will hide our imperfections from our sight,
For nothing can be angry or astray,
No man unpopular, lonely, or beset,
Where half a yellow moon hangs from a cloud.

Spinning however and balled up in space
All hearts, desires, pewter and honeysuckle,
What can be known of the individual face?
To the continual drum-beat of the blood
Mesh sea and mountain recollection, flame,
Motives in the corridor, touch by night,
Violent touch, and violence in rooms;
How shall we reconcile in any light
This blow and the relations that it wrecked?
Crescent the pressures on the singular act
Freeze it at last into its season, place,
Until the flood and disorder of Spring.
To Easterfield the court's best bore, defining
Space tied into a sailor's reef, our praise:
He too is useful, he is part of this,

Inimitable, tangible, post-human,
And Theo's disappointment has a place,
An item in that metamorphosis
The horrible coquetry of aging women.
Our superstitious barnacle our eyes
To the tide, the coming good; or has it come?—
Insufficient upon the beaches of the world
To drown that complex and that bestial drum.

Triumphant animal,—upon the rest
Bearing down hard, brooding, come to announce
The causes and directions of all this
Biting and breeding,—how will all your sons
Discover what you, assisted or alone,
Staring and sweating for seventy years,
Could never discover, the thing itself?
                                    Your fears,
Fidelity, and dandelions grown
As big as elephants, your morning lust
Can neither name nor control. No time for shame,
Whippoorwill calling, excrement falling, time
Rushes like a madman forward. Nothing can be known.

Desires of Men and Women

Exasperated, worn, you conjure a mansion,
The absolute butlers in the spacious hall,
Old silver, lace, and privacy, a house
Where nothing has for years been out of place,
Neither shoe-horn nor affection been out of place,
Breakfast in summer on the eastern terrace,
All justice and all grace.

                At the reception
Most beautifully you conduct yourselves—
Expensive and accustomed, bow, speak French,
That Cinquecento miniature recall
The Duke presented to your great-grandmother—

And none of us, my dears, would dream of you
The half-lit and lascivious apartments
That are in fact your goal, for which you'd do
Murder if you had not your cowardice
To prop the law; or dream of you the rooms,
Glaring and inconceivably vulgar,
Where now you are, where now you wish for life,
Whence you project your naked fantasies.

The Moon and the Night and the Men

On the night of the Belgian surrender the moon rose
Late, a delayed moon, and a violent moon
For the English or the American beholder;
The French beholder. It was a cold night,
People put on their wraps, the troops were cold
No doubt, despite the calendar, no doubt
Numbers of refugees coughed, and the sight
Or sound of some killed others. A cold night.

On Outer Drive there was an accident:
A stupid well-intentioned man turned sharp
Right and abruptly he became an angel
Fingering an unfamiliar harp,
Or screamed in hell, or was nothing at all.
Do not imagine this is unimportant.
He was a part of the night, part of the land,
Part of the bitter and exhausted ground
Out of which memory grows.

                              Michael and I
Stared at each other over chess, and spoke
As little as possible, and drank and played.
The chessmen caught in the European eye,
Neither of us I think had a free look
Although the game was fair. The move one made
It was difficult at last to keep one's mind on.
'. . . hurt and unhappy' said the man in London.
We said to each other, The time is coming near
When none shall have books or music, none his dear,
And only a fool will speak aloud his mind.
History is approaching a speechless end,
As Henry Adams said. Adams was right.

All this occurred on the night when Leopold
Fulfilled the treachery four years before
Begun—or was he well-intentioned, more
Roadmaker to hell than king? At any rate,
The moon came up late and the night was cold,
Many men died—although we know the fate
Of none, nor of anyone, and the war
Goes on, and the moon in the breast of man is cold.

The Ball Poem

What is the boy now, who has lost his ball,
What, what is he to do? I saw it go
Merrily bouncing, down the street, and then
Merrily over—there it is in the water!
No use to say 'O there are other balls':
An ultimate shaking grief fixes the boy
As he stands rigid, trembling, staring down
All his young days into the harbour where
His ball went. I would not intrude on him,
A dime, another ball, is worthless. Now
He senses first responsibility
In a world of possessions. People will take balls,
Balls will be lost always, little boy,
And no one buys a ball back. Money is external.
He is learning, well behind his desperate eyes,
The epistemology of loss, how to stand up
Knowing what every man must one day know
And most know many days, how to stand up.
And gradually light returns to the street,
A whistle blows, the ball is out of sight,
Soon part of me will explore the deep and dark
Floor of the harbour . . I am everywhere,
I suffer and move, my mind and my heart move
With all that move me, under the water
Or whistling, I am not a little boy.

Canto Amor

Dream in a dream the heavy soul somewhere
struck suddenly & dark down to its knees.
A griffin sighs off in the orphic air.

If (Unknown Majesty) I not confess
praise for the wrack the rock the live sailor
under the blue sea,—yet I may You bless

always for hér, in fear & joy for hér
whose gesture summons ever when I grieve
me back and is my mage and minister.

—Muses: whose worship I may never leave
but for this pensive woman, now I dare,
teach me her praise! with her my praise receive.—

Three years already of the round world's war
had rolled by stoned & disappointed eyes
when she and I came where we were made for.

Pale as a star lost in returning skies,
more beautiful than midnight stars more frail
she moved towards me like chords, a sacrifice;

entombed in body trembling through the veil
arm upon arm, learning our ancient wound,
we see our one soul heal, recovering pale.

Then priestly sanction, then the drop of sound.
Quickly part to the cavern ever warm
deep from the march, body to body bound

descend (my soul) out of dismantling storm
into the darkness where the world is made.
. . Come back to the bright air. Love is multiform.

Heartmating hesitating unafraid
although incredulous, she seemed to fill
the lilac shadow with light wherein she played,

whom sorry childhood had made sit quite still,
an orphan silence, unregarded sheen,
listening for any small soft note, not hopeful:

caricature: as once a maiden Queen,
flowering power comeliness kindness grace,
shattered her mirror, wept, would not be seen.

These pities moved. Also above her face
serious or flushed, swayed her fire-gold
not earthly hair, now moonless to unlace,

resistless flame, now in a sun more cold
great shells to whorl about each secret ear,
mysterious histories, white shores, unfold.

New musics! One the music that we hear,
this is the music which the masters make
out of their minds, profound solemn & clear.

And then the other music, in whose sake
all men perceive a gladness but we are drawn
less for that joy than utterly to take

our trial, naked in the music's vision,
the flowing ceremony of trouble and light,
all Loves becoming, none to flag upon.

Such Mozart made,—an ear so delicate
he fainted at a trumpet-call, a child
so delicate. So merciful that sight,

so stern, we follow rapt, who ran a-wild.
Marriage is the second music, and thereof
we hear what we can bear, faithful & mild.

Therefore the streaming torches in the grove
through dark or bright, swiftly & now more near
cherish a festival of anxious love.

Dance for this music, Mistress to music dear,
more, that storm worries the disordered wood
grieving the midnight of my thirtieth year

and only the trial of our music should
still this irresolute air, only your voice
spelling the tempest may compel our good:

Sigh then beyond my song: whirl & rejoice!

The Song of the Demented Priest

I put those things there. — See them burn.
The emerald the azure and the gold
Hiss and crack, the blues & greens of the world
As if I were tired. Someone interferes
Everywhere with me. The clouds, the clouds are torn
In ways I do not understand or love.

Licking my long lips, I looked upon God
And he flamed and he was friendlier
Than you were, and he was small. Showing me
Serpents and thin flowers; these were cold.
Dominion waved & glittered like the flare
From ice under a small sun. I wonder.

Afterward the violent and formal dancers
Came out, shaking their pithless heads.
I would instruct them but I cannot now, —
Because of the elements. They rise and move,
I nod a dance and they dance in the rain
In my red coat. I am the king of the dead.

The Song of the Tortured Girl

After a little I could not have told—
But no one asked me this—why I was there.
I asked. The ceiling of that place was high
And there were sudden noises, which I made.
I must have stayed there a long time today:
My cup of soup was gone when they brought me back.

Often 'Nothing worse now can come to us'
I thought, the winter the young men stayed away,
My uncle died, and mother cracked her crutch.
And then the strange room where the brightest light
Does not shine on the strange men: shines on me.
I feel them stretch my youth and throw a switch.

Through leafless branches the sweet wind blows
Making a mild sound, softer than a moan;
High in a pass once where we put our tent,
Minutes I lay awake to hear my joy.
—I no longer remember what they want.—
Minutes I lay awake to hear my joy.

The Lightning

Sick with the lightning lay my sister-in-law,
Concealing it from her children, when I came.
What I could, did, helpless with what I saw.

Analysands all, and the rest ought to be,
The friends my innocence cherished, and you and I,
Darling, — the friends I qualm and cherish and see.

. . The fattest nation! — wé do not thrive fat
But facile in the scale with all we rise
And shift a breakfast, and there is shame in that.

And labour sweats with vice at the top, and two
Bullies are bristling. What he thought who thinks?
It is difficult to say what one will do.

Obstinate, gleams from the black world the gay and fair,
My love loves choclate, she loves also me,
And the lightning dances, but I cannot despair.

Whether There Is Sorrow in the Demons

Near the top a bad turn some dare. Well,
The horse swerves and creams, his eyes pop,
Feet feel air, the firm winds prop
Jaws wide wider until
Through great teeth rider greets the smiles of Hell.

Thick night, where the host's thews crack like thongs
A welcome, curving abrupt on cheek & neck.
No wing swings over once to check
Lick of their fire's tongues,
Whip & chuckle, hoarse insulting songs.

Powers immortal, fixed, intractable.
Only the lost soul jerks whom they joy hang:
Clap of remorse, and tang and fang
More frightful than the drill
An outsize dentist scatters down a skull;

Nostalgia rips him swinging. Fast in malice
How may his masters mourn, how ever yearn
The frore pride wherein they burn?
God's fire. To what *qui tollis*
Stone-tufted ears prick back towards the bright Palace?

Whence Lucifer shone Lucifer's friends hail
The scourge of choice made at the point of light
Destined into eternal night;
Motionless to fulfil
Their least, their envy looks up dense and pale.

New Year's Eve

The grey girl who had not been singing stopped,
And a brave new no-sound blew through acrid air.
I set my drink down, hard. Somebody slapped
Somebody's second wife somewhere,
Wheeling away to long to be alone.
I see the dragon of years is almost done,
Its claws loosen, its eyes
Crust now with tears & lust and a scale of lies.

A whisky-listless and excessive saint
Was expounding his position, whom I hung
Boy-glad in glowing heaven: he grows faint:
Hearing what song the sirens sung,
Sidelong he web-slid and some rich prose spun.
The tissue golden of the gifts undone
Surpassed the gifts. Miss Weirs
Whispers to me her international fears.

Intelligentsia milling. In a semi-German
(Our loss of Latin fractured how far our fate,—
Disinterested once, linkage once like a sermon)
I struggle to articulate
Why it is our promise breaks in pieces early.
The Muses' visitants come soon, go surly
With liquor & mirrors away
In this land wealthy & casual as a holiday.

Whom the Bitch winks at. Most of us are linsey-
woolsey workmen, grandiose, and slack.
On m'analyse, the key to secrets. Kinsey
Shortly will tell us sharply back
Habits we stuttered. How revive to join
(Great evils grieve beneath: eye Caesar's coin)
And lure a while more home
The vivid wanderers, uneasy with our shame?

24

Priests of the infinite! ah, not for long.
The dove whispers, and diminishes
Up the blue leagues. And no doubt we heard wrong—
Wax of our lives collects & dulls; but was
What we heard hurried as we memorized,
Or brightened, or adjusted? Undisguised
We pray our tongues & fingers
Record the strange word that blows suddenly and lingers.

Imagine a patience in the works of love
Luck sometimes visits. Ages we have sighed,
And cleave more sternly to a music of
Even this sore word 'genocide'.
Each to his own! Clockless & thankless dream
And labour Makers, being what we seem.
Soon O enough we turn
Our tools in; brownshirt Time chiefly our works will burn.

I remember: white fine flour everywhere whirled
Ceaselessly, wheels rolled, a slow thunder boomed,
And there were snowy men in the mill-world
With sparkling eyes, light hair uncombed,
And one of them was humming an old song,
Sack upon sack grew portly, until strong
Arms moved them on, by pairs,
And then the bell clanged and they ran like hares.

Scotch in his oxter, my Retarded One
Blows in before the midnight; freezing slush
Stamps off, off. Worst of years! . . no matter, begone;
Your slash and spells (in the sudden hush)
We see now we had to suffer some day, so
I cross the dragon with a blessing, low,
While the black blood slows. Clock-wise,
We clasp upon the stroke, kissing with happy cries.

Of 1947

The Dispossessed

'and something that . . that is theirs—no longer ours'
stammered to me the Italian page. A wood
seeded & towered suddenly. I understood.—

The Leading Man's especially, and the Juvenile Lead's,
and the Leading Lady's thigh that switches & warms,
and their grimaces, and their flying arms:

our arms, our story. Every seat was sold.
A crone met in a clearing sprouts a beard
and has a tirade. Not a word we heard.

Movement of stone within a woman's heart,
abrupt & dominant. They gesture how
fings really are. Rarely a child sings now.

My harpsichord weird as a koto drums
adagio for twilight, for the storm-worn dove
no more de-iced, and the spidery business of love.

The Juvenile Lead's the Leader's arm, one arm
running the whole bole, branches, roots, (O watch)
and the faceless fellow waving from her crotch,

Stalin-unanimous! who procured a vote
and care not use it, who have kept an eye
and care not use it, percussive vote, clear eye.

That which a captain and a weaponeer
one day and one more day did, we did, *ach*
we did not, *They* did . . cam slid, the great lock

lodged, and no soul of us all was near was near,—
an evil sky (where the umbrella bloomed)
twirled its mustaches, hissed, the ingenue fumed,

poor virgin, and no hero rides. The race
is done. Drifts through, between the cold black trunks,
the peachblow glory of the perishing sun

in empty houses where old things take place.

Venice, 182—

White & blue my breathing lady leans
across me in the first light, so we kiss.
The corners of her eyes are white. I miss.
renew. She means
to smother me thro' years of this.

Hell chill young widows in the heel of night—
perduring loves, melody's thrusting, press
flush with the soft skin, whence they sprung! back. Less
ecstasy might
save us for speech & politeness.

I hear her howl now, and I slam my eyes
against the glowing face. Foul morning-cheese
stands fair compared to love. On waspish knees
our pasts surprise
and plead us livid. Now she frees

a heavy lock was pulling . . I kiss it,
lifting my hopeless lids—and all trace
of passion's vanisht from her eyes & face,
the lip I bit
is bluer, a blackhead at the base

of her smooth nose looks sullenly at me,
we look at each other in entire despair,
her eyes are swimming by mine, and I swear
sobbing quickly
we are in love. The light hurts. 'There . .'

from **The Black Book (i)**

Grandfather, sleepless in a room upstairs,
seldom came down; so when they tript him down
we wept. The blind light sang about his ears,
later we heard. Brother had pull. In pairs
he, some, slept upon stone.
Later they stamped him down in mud.
The windlass drew him silly & odd-eyed, blood
broke from his ears before they quit.
Before they trucked him home they cleaned him up somewhat.

Only the loose eyes' glaze they could not clean
and soon he died. He howled a night and shook
our teeth before the end; we breathed again
when he stopt. Abraham, what we have seen
write, I beg, in your Book.
No more the solemn and high bells
call to our pall; we call or gibber; Hell's
irritable & treacherous
despairs here here (not him) reach now to shatter us.

Not To Live

It kissed us, soft, to cut our throats, this coast,
like a malice of the lazy King. I hunt,
 & hunt! but find here what to kill?—nothing is blunt,
but phantoming uneases I find. Ghost
on ghost precedes of all most scared us, most
we fled. Howls fail upon this secret, far air: grunt,
shaming for food; you must. I love the King
 & it was not I who strangled at the toast
but a flux of a free & dying adjutant:
God be with him. He & God be with us all,
for we are not to live. I cannot wring,
like laundry, blue my soul—indecisive thing . .
From undergrowth & over odd birds call
and who would starv'd so survive? God save the King.

JAMESTOWN 1957

33

A Sympathy, A Welcome

Feel for your bad fall how could I fail,
poor Paul, who had it so good.
I can offer you only: this world like a knife.
Yet you'll get to know your mother
and humourless as you do look you will laugh
and all the others
will *not* be fierce to you, and loverhood
will swing your soul like a broken bell
deep in a forsaken wood, poor Paul,
whose wild bad father loves you well.

Note to Wang Wei

How could you be so happy, now some thousand years
dishevelled, puffs of dust?
It leaves me uneasy at last,
your poems teaze me to the verge of tears
and your fate. It makes me think.
It makes me long for mountains & blue waters.
Makes me wonder how much to allow.
(I'm reconfirming, God of bolts & bangs,
of fugues & bucks, whose rocket burns & sings.)
I wish we could meet for a drink
in a 'freedom from ten thousand matters'.
Be dust myself pretty soon; not now.

BERRYMAN'S SONNETS
(1952,1967)

9

Great citadels whereon the gold sun falls
Miss you O Lise sequestered to the West
Which wears you Mayday lily at its breast,
Part and not part, proper to balls and brawls,
Plains, cities, or the yellow shore, not false
Anywhere, free, native and Danishest
Profane and elegant flower, — whom suggest
Frail and not frail, blond rocks and madrigals.

Once in the car (cave of our radical love)
Your darker hair I saw than golden hair
Above your thighs whiter than white-gold hair,
And where the dashboard lit faintly your least
Enlarged scene, O the midnight bloomed . . the East
Less gorgeous, wearing you like a long white glove!

12

Mutinous armed & suicidal grind
Fears on desires, a clutter humps a track,
The body of expectation hangs down slack
Untidy black; my love sweats like a rind;
Parrots are yattering up the cagy mind,
Jerking their circles . . you stood, a week back,
By, I saw your foot with half my eye, I lack
You . . the damned female's yellow head swings blind.

Cageless they'd grapple. O where, whose Martini
Grows sweeter with my torment, wrung on toward
The insomnia of eternity, loud graves!
Hölderlin on his tower sang like the sea
More you adored that day than your harpsichord,
Troubled and drumming, tempting and empty waves.

13

I lift—lift you five States away your glass,
Wide of this bar you never graced, where none
Ever I know came, where what work is done
Even by these men I know not, where a brass
Police-car sign peers in, wet strange cars pass,
Soiled hangs the rag of day out over this town,
A juke-box brains air where I drink alone,
The spruce barkeep sports a toupee alas—

My glass I lift at six o'clock, my darling,
As you plotted . . Chinese couples shift in bed,
We shared today not even filthy weather,
Beasts in the hills their tigerish love are snarling,
Suddenly they clash, I blow my short ash red,
Grey eyes light! and we have our drink together.

21

Whom undone David into the dire van sent
I'd see as far. I can't dislike that man,
Grievously and intensely like him even,
Envy nor jealousy admit, consent
Neither to the night of rustlers I frequent
Nor to this illness dreams them; but I can,
Only, that which we must: bright as a pan
Our love gleams, empty almost empty—lent.

. . Did he, or not, see? I stood close to you
But our lips had broken and you could reply . .
And *is* he clement? does he give us rope?
It is the owner drives one crazy, who
Came, or luck brought him, first; a police spy;
A kind and good man; with a gun; hunts hope.

If not white shorts — then in a princess gown
Where gaslights pierce the mist I'd have your age,
Young in a grey gown, blonde and royal, rage
Of handlebars at Reisenweber's, frown
Or smile to quell or rally half the town,
To polka partners mad, to flout the stage,
To pale The Lily to an average
Woman, looking up from your champagne, or down.

Myself, ascotted, still dumb as a mome
Drinking your eyes . . No Bill comes by to cadge
A Scotch in Rector's, waving his loose tongue.
I tip my skimmer to your friend who clung
Too long, blue-stocking cracked on the *Red Badge*
Stevie's becoming known for . . We drive home.

Sometimes the night echoes to prideless wailing
Low as I hunch home late and fever-tired,
Near you not, nearing the sharer I desired,
Toward whom till now I sailed back; but that sailing
Yaws, from the cabin orders like a failing
Dribble, the stores disordered and then fired
Skid wild, the men are glaring, the mate has wired
Hopeless: locked in, and humming, the Captain's nailing
A false log to the lurching table. Lies
And passion sing in the cabin on the voyage home,
The burgee should fly Jolly Roger: wind
Madness like the tackle of a crane (outcries
Ascend) around to heave him from the foam
Irresponsible, since all the stars rain blind.

34

'I *couldn't leave* you' you confessed next day.
Our law too binds. Grossly however bound
And jacketed apart, ensample-wound,
We come so little and can so little stay
Together, what can we know? Anything may
Amaze me: this did. Ah, to work underground
Slowly and wholly in your vein profound . .
Or like some outcast ancient Jew to say:

'There *is* Judaea: in it Jerusalem:
In that the Temple: in the Temple's inmost
Holy of holies hides the invisible Ark —
There nothing — there all — vast wing beating dark —
Voiceless, the terrible I AM — the lost
Tables of stone with the Law graved on them!'

37

Sigh as it ends . . . I keep an eye on your
Amour with Scotch, — too *cher* to consummate;
Faster your disappearing beer than late-
ly mine; your naked passion for the floor;
Your hollow leg; your hanker for one more
Dark as the Sundam Trench; how you dilate
Upon psychotics of this class, collate
Stages, and . . how long since you, well, *forbore.*

Ah, but the high fire sings on to be fed
Whipping our darkness by the lifting sea
A while, O darling drinking like a clock.
The tide comes on: spare, Time, from what you spread
Her story, — tilting a frozen Daiquiri,
Blonde, barefoot, beautiful,
        flat on the bare floor rivetted to Bach.

65

Once when they found me, some refrain *'Quoi faire?'*
Striking my hands, they say repeatedly
I muttered; although I could hear and see
I knew no one. — I am silent in my chair,
And stronger and more cold is my despair
At last, for I have come into a country
Whose vivid Queen upon no melody
Admits me. *Manchmal glaub ich, ich kann nicht mehr.*

Song follows song, the chatterer to the fire
Would follow soon . . Deep in Ur's royal pits
Sit still the courtly bodies, a little bowl
By each, attired to voluntary blitz . .
In Shub-ad's grave the fingers of a girl
Were touching still, when they found her, the strings of her lyre.

71

Our Sunday morning when dawn-priests were applying
Wafer and wine to the human wound, we laid
Ourselves to cure ourselves down: I'm afraid
Our vestments wanted, but Francis' friends were crying
In the nave of pines, sun-satisfied, and flying
Subtle as angels about the barricade
Boughs made over us, deep in a bed half made
Needle-soft, half the sea of our simultaneous dying.

'Death is the mother of beauty.' Awry no leaf
Shivering with delight, we die to be well . .
Careless with sleepy love, so long unloving.
What if our convalescence must be brief
As we are, the matin meet the passing bell? . .
About our pines our sister, wind, is moving.

75

Swarthy when young; who took the tonsure; sign,
His coronation, wangled, his name re-said
For euphony; off to courts fluttered, and fled;
Professorships refused; upon one line
Worked years; and then that genial concubine.
Seventy springs he read, and wrote, and read.
On the day of the year his people found him dead
I read his story. Anew I studied mine.

Also there was Laura and three-seventeen
Sonnets to something like her . . twenty-one years . .
He never touched her. Swirl our crimes and crimes.
Gold-haired (too), dark-eyed, ignorant of rimes
Was she? Virtuous? The old brume seldom clears.
—Two guilty and crepe-yellow months
     Lise! be our bright surviving actual scene.

79

I dreamt he drove me back to the asylum
Straight after lunch; we stood then at one end,
A sort of cafeteria behind, my friend
Behind me, nuts in groups about the room;
A dumbwaiter with five shelves was waiting (some-
thing's missing here) to take me up—I bend
And lift a quart of milk to hide and tend,
Take with me. Everybody is watching, dumb.

I try to put it first among some worm-
shot volumes of the N.E.D. I had
On the top shelf—then somewhere else . . slowly
Lise comes up in a matron's uniform
And with a look (I saw once) infinitely sad
In her grey eyes takes it away from me.

97

I say *I laid siege — you enchanted me* . .
Magic and warfare, faithful metaphors
As when their paleolithic woods and tors
The hunter and the witchwife roamed, half free,
Half to the Provider and the Mystery-
riddler bound: the kill, the spell: your languors
I wag my wolf's tail to — without remorse? —
You shudder as I'd pierce you where I knee

I . . Only we little wished, or you to charm
Or I to make you shudder, you to wreck
Or I to hum you daring on my arm.
Abrupt as a dogfight, the air full of
Tails and teeth — the meshing of a trek —
All this began: knock-down-and-drag-out love.

106

Began with swirling, blind, unstilled oh still, —
The tide had set in toward the western door
And I was working with the tide, I bore
My panful of reflexion firm, until
A voice arrested me, — body, and will,
And panful, wheeled and spilt, tempted nerves tore,
And all uncome time blackened like the core
Of an apple on through man's heart moving still . .

At nine o'clock and thirty Thursday night,
In Nineteen XXXX, February
Twice-ten-day, by a doorway in McIntosh,
So quietly neither the rip's cold slosh
Nor the meshing of great wheels warned me, unwary,
An enigmatic girl smiled out my sight.

Ménage à trois, like Tristan's, — difficult! . .
The convalescent Count; his mistress; fast
The wiry wild arthritic young fantast
In love with her, his genius occult,
His weakness blazing, ugly, an insult
A salutation; in his yacht they assed
Up and down the whole coast six months . . last
It couldn't: . . the pair to Paris. Chaos, result.

Well — but four worse!! . . all four, marvellous friends —
Some horse-shit here, eh? — You admitted it,
Come, you did once . . and we *are friends*, I say. —
'La Cuchiani aima Tristan, mais . .'
(The biographer says) *unscrupulous* a bit,
Or utterly . . . There, of course, the resemblance ends.

I break my pace now for a sonic boom,
the future's with & in us. I sit fired
but comes on strong with the fire fatigue: I'm tired.
'I'd drive my car across the living-room
if I could get it inside the house.' You loom
less, less than before when your voice choired
into my transept hear I now it, not expired
but half-dead with exhaustion, like Mr Bloom.

Dazzle, before I abandon you, my eyes,
my eyes which I need for journeys difficult
in which case it may be said that I survive you.
Your voice continues, with its lows & highs,
and I am a willing accomplice in the cult
and every word that I   have gasped of you is true.

HOMAGE TO
MISTRESS BRADSTREET
(1953)

Homage to Mistress Bradstreet

1

The Governor your husband lived so long
moved you not, restless, waiting for him? Still,
you were a patient woman—
I seem to see you pause here still:
Sylvester, Quarles, in moments odd you pored
before a fire at, bright eyes on the Lord,
all the children still.
'Simon . .' Simon will listen while you read a Song.

2

Outside the New World winters in grand dark
white air lashing high thro' the virgin stands
foxes down foxholes sigh,
surely the English heart quails, stunned.
I doubt if Simon than this blast, that sea,
spares from his rigour for your poetry
more. We are on each other's hands
who care. Both of our worlds unhanded us. Lie stark,

3

thy eyes look to me mild. Out of maize & air
your body's made, and moves. I summon, see,
from the centuries it.
I think you won't stay. How do we
linger, diminished, in our lovers' air,
implausibly visible, to whom, a year,
years, over interims; or not;
to a long stranger; or not; shimmer and disappear.

4

Jaw-ript, rot with its wisdom, rending then;
then not. When the mouth dies, who misses you?
Your master never died,   .
Simon ah thirty years past you—
Pockmarkt & westward staring on a haggard deck
it seems I find you, young. I come to check,
I come to stay with you,
and the Governor, & Father, & Simon, & the huddled men.

5

By the week we landed we were, most, used up.
Strange ships across us, after a fortnight's winds
unfavouring, frightened us;
bone-sad cold, sleet, scurvy; so were ill
many as one day we could have no sermons;
broils, quelled; a fatherless child unkennelled; vermin
crowding & waiting: waiting.
And the day itself he leapt ashore young Henry Winthrop

6

(delivered from the waves; because he found
off their wigwams, sharp-eyed, a lone canoe
across a tidal river,
that water glittered fair & blue
& narrow, none of the other men could swim
and the plantation's prime theft up to him,
shouldered on a glad day
hard on the glorious feasting of thanksgiving) drowned.

7

How long with nothing in the ruinous heat,
clams & acorns stomaching, distinction perishing,
at which my heart rose,
with brackish water, we would sing.
When whispers knew the Governor's last bread
was browning in his oven, we were discourag'd.
The Lady Arbella dying—
dyings—at which my heart   rose, but I did submit.

That beyond the Atlantic wound our woes enlarge
is hard, hard that starvation burnishes our fear,
but I do gloss for You.
Strangers & pilgrims fare we here,
declaring we seek a City. Shall we be deceived?
I know whom I have trusted, & whom I have believed.
and that he is able to
keep   that I have committed to his charge.

9

Winter than summer worse, that first, like a file
on a quick, or the poison suck of a thrilled tooth;
and still we may unpack.
Wolves & storms among, uncouth
board-pieces, boxes, barrels vanish, grow
houses, rise. Motes that hop in sunlight slow
indoors, and I am Ruth
away: open my mouth, my eyes wet; I wóuld smile:

vellum I palm, and dream. Their forest dies
to greensward, privets, elms & towers, whence
a nightingale is throbbing.
Women sleep sound. I was happy once . .
(Something keeps on not happening; I shrink?)
These minutes all their passions & powers sink
and I am not one chance
for an unknown cry or a flicker of unknown eyes.

11

Chapped souls ours, by the day Spring's strong winds swelled,
Jack's pulpits arched, more glad. The shawl I pinned
flaps like a shooting soul
might in such weather Heaven send.
Succumbing half, in spirit, to a salmon sash
I prod the nerveless novel succotash —
I must be disciplined,
in arms, against that one, and our dissidents, and myself.

12

Versing, I shroud among the dynasties;
quaternion on quaternion, tireless I phrase
anything past, dead, far,
sacred, for a barbarous place.
— To please your wintry father? all this bald
abstract didactic rime I read appalled
harassed for your fame
mistress neither of fiery nor velvet verse, on your knees

hopeful & shamefast, chaste, laborious, odd,
whom the sea tore. — The damned roar with loss,
so they hug & are mean
with themselves, and I cannot be thus.
Why then do I repine, sick, bad, to long
after what must not be? I lie wrong
once more. For at fourteen
I found my heart more carnal and sitting loose from God,

vanity & the follies of youth took hold of me;
then the pox blasted, when the Lord returned.
That year for my sorry face
so-much-older Simon burned,
so Father smiled, with love. Their will be done.
He to me ill lingeringly, learning to shun
a bliss, a lightning blood
vouchsafed, what did seem life. I kissed his Mystery.

Drydust in God's eye the aquavivid skin
of Simon snoring lit with fountaining dawn
when my eyes unlid, sad.
John Cotton shines on Boston's sin —
I ám drawn, in pieties that seem
the weary drizzle of an unremembered dream.
Women have gone mad
at twenty-one. Ambition mines, atrocious, in.

Food endless, people few, all to be done.
As pippins roast, the question of the wolves
turns & turns.
Fangs of a wolf will keep, the neck
round of a child, that child brave. I remember who
in meeting smiled & was punisht, and I know who
whispered & was stockt.
We lead a thoughtful life. But Boston's cage we shun.

17

The winters close, Springs open, no child stirs
under my withering heart, O seasoned heart
God grudged his aid.
All things else soil like a shirt.
Simon is much away. My executive stales.
The town came through for the cartway by the pales,
but my patience is short,
I revolt from, I am like, these savage foresters

whose passionless dicker in the shade, whose glance
impassive & scant, belie their murderous cries
when quarry seems to show.
Again I must have been wrong, twice.
Unwell in a new way. Can that begin?
God brandishes. O love, O I love. Kin,
gather. My world is strange
and merciful, ingrown months, blessing a swelling trance.

19

So squeezed, wince you I scream? I love you & hate
off with you. Ages! *Useless*. Below my waist
he has me in Hell's vise.   -
Stalling. He let go. Come back: brace
me somewhere. No. No. Yes! everything down
hardens I press with horrible joy down
my back cracks like a wrist
shame I am voiding oh behind it is too late

20

hide me forever I work thrust I must free
now I all muscles & bones concentrate
what is living from dying?
Simon I must leave you so untidy
Monster you are killing me Be sure
I'll have you later Women do endure
I can *can* no longer
and it passes the wretched trap whelming and I am me

21

drencht & powerful, I did it with my body!
One proud tug greens Heaven. Marvellous,
unforbidding Majesty.
Swell, imperious bells. I fly.
Mountainous, woman not breaks and will bend:
sways God nearby: anguish comes to an end.
Blossomed Sarah, and I
blossom. Is that thing alive? I hear a famisht howl.

Beloved household, I am Simon's wife,
and the mother of Samuel—whom greedy yet I miss
out of his kicking place.
More in some ways I feel at a loss,
freer. Cantabanks & mummers, nears
longing for you. Our chopping scores my ears,
our costume bores my eyes.
St. George to the good sword, rise! chop-logic's rife

& fever & Satan & Satan's ancient fere.
Pioneering is not feeling well,
not Indians, beasts.
Not all their riddling can forestall
one leaving. Sam, your uncle has had to
go fróm us to live with God. 'Then Aunt went too?'
Dear, she does wait still.
Stricken: 'Oh. Then he takes us one by one.' My dear.

24

Forswearing it otherwise, they starch their minds.
Folkmoots, & blether, blether. John Cotton rakes
to the synod of Cambridge.
Down from my body my legs flow,
out from it arms wave, on it my head shakes.
Now Mistress Hutchinson rings forth a call—
should she? many creep out at a broken wall—
affirming the Holy Ghost
dwells in one justified. Factioning passion blinds

all to all her good, all — can she be exiled?
Bitter sister, victim! I miss you.
— I miss you, Anne,
day or night weak as a child,
tender & empty, doomed, quick to no tryst.
— I hear you. Be kind, you who leaguer
my image in the mist.
— Be kind you, to one unchained eager far & wild

and if, O my love, my heart is breaking, please
neglect my cries and I will spare you. Deep
in Time's grave, Love's, you lie still.
Lie still. — Now? That happy shape
my forehead had under my most long, rare,
ravendark, hidden, soft bodiless hair
you award me still.
You must not love me, but   I do not bid you cease.

Veiled my eyes, attending. How can it be I?
Moist, with parted lips, I listen, wicked.
I shake in the morning & retch.
Brood I do on myself naked.
A fading world I dust, with fingers new.
— I have earned the right to be alone with you.
— What right can that be?
Convulsing, if you love, enough, like a sweet lie.

Not that, I know, you can. This cratered skin,
like the crabs & shells of my Palissy ewer, touch!
Oh, you do, you do?
Falls on me what I like a witch,
for lawless holds, annihilations of law
which Time and he and man abhor, foresaw:
sharper than what my Friend
brought me for my revolt when I moved smooth & thin,

faintings black, rigour, chilling, brown
parching, back, brain burning, the grey pocks
itch, a manic stench
of pustules snapping, pain floods the palm,
sleepless, or a red shaft with a dreadful start
rides at the chapel, like a slipping heart.
My soul strains in one qualm
ah but *this* is not to save me but to throw me down.

And out of this I lull. It lessens. Kiss me.
That once. As sings out up in sparkling dark
a trail of a star & dies,
while the breath flutters, sounding, mark,
so shorn ought such caresses to us be
who, deserving nothing, flush and flee
the darkness of that light,
a lurching frozen from a warm dream. Talk to me.

31

—It is Spring's New England. Pussy willows wedge
up in the wet. Milky crestings, fringed
yellow, in heaven, eyed
by the melting hand-in-hand or mere
desirers single, heavy-footed, rapt,
make surge poor human hearts. Venus is trapt—
the hefty pike shifts, sheer—
in Orion blazing. Warblings, odours, nudge to an edge—

32

—Ravishing, ha, what crouches outside ought,
flamboyant, ill, angelic. Often, now,
I am afraid of you.
I am a sobersides; I know.
I *want* to take you for my lover.—Do.
—I hear a madness. Harmless I to you
am not, not I?—No.
—I cannot but be. Sing a concord of our thought.

33

—Wan dolls in indigo on gold: refrain
my western lust. I am drowning in this past.
I lose sight of you
who mistress me from air. Unbraced
in delirium of the grand depths, giving away
haunters what kept me, I breathe solid spray.
—I am losing you!
Straiten me on.—I suffered living like a stain:

34

I trundle the bodies, on the iron bars,
over that fire backward & forth; they burn;
bits fall. I wonder if
I killed them. Women serve my turn.
—Dreams! You are good.—No.—Dense with hardihood
the wicked are dislodged, and lodged the good.
In green space we are safe.
God awaits us (but I am yielding) who Hell wars.

35

—I cannot feel myself God waits. He flies
nearer a kindly world; or he is flown.
One Saturday's rescue
won't show. Man is entirely alone
may be. I am a man of griefs & fits
trying to be my friend. And the brown smock splits,
down the pale flesh a gash
broadens and Time holds up your heart against my eyes.

36

—Hard and divided heaven! creases me. Shame
is failing. My breath is scented, and I throw
hostile glances towards God.
Crumpling plunge of a pestle, bray:
sin cross & opposite, wherein I survive
nightmares of Eden. Reaches foul & live
he for me, this soul
to crunch, a minute tangle of eternal flame.

37

I fear Hell's hammer-wind. But fear does wane.
Death's blossoms grain my hair; I cannot live.
A black joy clashes
joy, in twilight. The Devil said
'I will deal toward her softly, and her enchanting cries
will fool the horns of Adam.' Father of lies,
a male great pestle smashes
small women swarming towards the mortar's rim in vain.

38

I see the cruel spread Wings black with saints!
Silky my breasts not his, mine, mine to withhold
or tender, tender.
I am sifting, nervous, and bold.
The light is changing. Surrender this loveliness
you cannot make me do. *But* I will. Yes.
What horror, down stormy air,
warps towards me? My threatening promise faints

39

torture me, Father, lest not I be thine!
Tribunal terrible & pure, my God,
mercy for him and me.
Faces half-fanged, Christ drives abroad,
and though the crop hopes, Jane is so slipshod
I cry. Evil dissolves, & love, like foam;
that love. Prattle of children powers me home,
my heart claps like the swan's
under a frenzy of *who* love me & who shine.

As a canoe slides by on one strong stroke
hope his hélp not I, who do hardly bear
his gift still. But whisper
I am not utterly. I pare
an apple for my pipsqueak Mercy and
she runs & all need naked apples, fanned
their tinier envies.
Vomitings, trots, rashes. Can be hope a cloak?

for the man with cropt ears glares. My fingers tighten
my skirt. I pass. Alas! I pity all.
Shy, shy, with mé, Dorothy.
Moonrise, and frightening hoots. 'Mother,
how *long* will I be dead?' Our friend the owl
vanishes, darling, but your homing soul
retires on Heaven, Mercy:
not we one instant die, only our dark does lighten.

When by me in the dusk my child sits down
I am myself. Simon, if it's that loose,
let me wiggle it out.
You'll get a bigger one there, & bite.
How they loft, how their sizes delight and grate.
The proportioned, spiritless poems accumulate.
And they publish them
away in brutish London, for a hollow crown.

Father is not himself. He keeps his bed,
and threw a saffron scum Thursday. God-forsaken words
escaped him raving. Save,
Lord, thy servant zealous & just.
Sam he saw back from Harvard. He did scold
his secting enemies. His stomach is cold
while we drip, while
my baby John breaks out. O far from where he bred!

44

Bone of moaning: sung Where he has gone
a thousand summers by truth-hallowed souls;
be still. Agh, he is gone!
Where? I know. Beyond the shoal.
Still-all a Christian daughter grinds her teeth
a little. This our land has ghosted with
our dead: I am at home.
Finish, Lord, in me this work thou hast begun.

45

And they tower, whom the pear-tree lured
to let them fall, fierce mornings they reclined
down the brook-bank to the east
fishing for shiners with a crookt pin,
wading, dams massing, well, and Sam's to be
a doctor in Boston. After the divisive sea,
and death's first feast,
and the galled effort on the wilderness endured,

46

Arminians, and the King bore against us;
of an 'inward light' we hear with horror.
Whose fan is in his hand
and he will throughly purge his floor,
come towards mé. I have what licks the joints
and bites the heart, which winter more appoints.
Iller I, oftener.
Hard at the outset; in the ending thus hard, thus?

47

Sacred & unutterable Mind
flashing thorough the universe one thought,
I do wait without peace.
In the article of death I budge.
Eat my sore breath, Black Angel. Let me die.
Body a-drain, when will you be dry
and countenance my speed
to Heaven's springs? lest stricter writhings have me declined.

48

'What are those pictures in the air at night,
Mother?' Mercy did ask. Space charged with faces
day & night! I place
a goatskin's fetor, and sweat: fold me
in savoury arms. Something is shaking, wrong.
He smells the musket and lifts it. It is long.
It points at my heart.
Missed he must have. In the gross storm of sunlight

I sniff a fire burning without outlet,
consuming acrid its own smoke. It's me.
Ruined laughter sounds
outside. Ah but I waken, free.
And so I am about again. I hagged
a fury at the short maid, whom tongues tagged,
and I am sorry. Once
less I was anxious when more passioned to upset

the mansion & the garden & the beauty of God.
Insectile unreflective busyness
blunts & does amend.
Hangnails, piles, fibs, life's also.
But we are that from which draws back a thumb.
The seasons stream and, somehow, I am become
an old woman. It's so:
I look. I bear to look. Strokes once more his rod.

My window gives on the graves, in our great new house
(how many burned?) upstairs, among the elms.
I lie, & endure, & wonder.
A haze slips sometimes over my dreams
and holiness on horses' bells shall stand.
Wandering pacemaker, unsteadying friend,
in a redskin calm I wait:
beat when you will our end. Sinkings & droopings drowse.

They say thro' the fading winter Dorothy fails,
my second, who than I bore one more, nine;
and I see her inearthed. I linger.
Seaborn she wed knelt before Simon;
Simon I, and linger. Black-yellow seething, vast
it lies fróm me, mine: all they look aghast.
It will be a glorious arm.
Docile I watch. My wreckt chest hurts when Simon pales.

53

In the yellowing days your faces wholly fail,
at Fall's onset. Solemn voices fade.
I feel no coverlet.
Light notes leap, a beckon, swaying
the tilted, sickening ear within. I'll—I'll—
I am closed & coming. Somewhere! I defile
wide as a cloud, in a'cloud,
unfit, desirous, glad—even the singings veil—

54

—You are not ready? You áre ready. Pass,
as shadow gathers shadow in the welling night.
Fireflies of childhood torch
you down. We commit our sister down.
One candle mourn by, which a lover gave,
the use's edge and order of her grave.
Quiet? Moisture shoots.
Hungry throngs collect. They sword into the carcass.

55

Headstones stagger under great draughts of time
after heads pass out, and their world must reel
speechless, blind in the end
about its chilling star: thrift tuft,
whin cushion—nothing. Already with the wounded flying
dark air fills, I am a closet of secrets dying,
races murder, foxholes hold men,
reactor piles wage slow upon the wet brain rime.

56

I must pretend to leave you. Only you draw off
a benevolent phantom. I say you seem to me
drowned towns off England,
featureless as those myriads
who what bequeathed save fire-ash, fossils, burled
in the open river-drifts of the Old World?
Simon lived on for years.
I renounce not even ragged glances, small teeth, nothing,

57

O all your ages at the mercy of my loves
together lie at once, forever or
so long as I happen.
In the rain of pain & departure, still
Love has no body and presides the sun,
and elfs from silence melody. I run.
Hover, utter, still,
a sourcing   whom my lost candle like the firefly loves.

TO KATE, AND TO SAUL
'THOU DREWEST NEAR IN THE DAY'

'GO IN, BRACK MAN, DE DAY'S YO' OWN.'

. . . I AM THEIR MUSICK.
Lam. 3:63

BUT THERE IS ANOTHER METHOD.
Olive Schreiner

from
THE DREAM SONGS (1964,1968)

1

Huffy Henry hid   the day,
unappeasable Henry sulked.
I see his point,—a trying to put things over.
It was the thought that they thought
they could *do* it made Henry wicked & away.
But he should have come out and talked.

All the world like a woolen lover
once did seem on Henry's side.
Then came a departure.
Thereafter nothing fell out as it might or ought.
I don't see how Henry, pried
open for all the world to see, survived.

What he has now to say is a long
wonder the world can bear & be.
Once in a sycamore I was glad
all at the top, and I sang.
Hard on the land wears the strong sea
and empty grows every bed.

4

Filling her compact & delicious body
with chicken páprika, she glanced at me
twice.
Fainting with interest, I hungered back
and only the fact of her husband & four other people
kept me from springing on her

or falling at her little feet and crying
'You are the hottest one for years of night
Henry's dazed eyes
have enjoyed, Brilliance.' I advanced upon
(despairing) my spumoni. — Sir Bones: is stuffed,
de world, wif feeding girls.

— Black hair, complexion Latin, jewelled eyes
downcast . . . The slob beside her   feasts . . . What wonders is
she sitting on, over there?
The restaurant buzzes. She might as well be on Mars.
Where did it all go wrong? There ought to be a law against Henry.
— Mr. Bones: there is.

5

Henry sats in de bar & was odd,
off in the glass from the glass,
at odds wif de world & its god,
his wife is a complete nothing,
St Stephen
getting even.

Henry sats in de plane & was gay.
Careful Henry nothing said aloud
but where a Virgin out of cloud
to her Mountain dropt in light,
his thought made pockets & the plane buckt.
'Parm me, lady.' 'Orright.'

Henry lay in de netting, wild,
while the brainfever bird did scales;
Mr Heartbreak, the New Man,
come to farm a crazy land;
an image of the dead on the fingernail
of a newborn child.

6 A Capital at Wells

During the father's walking — how he look
down by now in soft boards, Henry, pass
and what he feel or no, who know? —
as during his broad father's, all the breaks
 & ill-lucks of a thriving pioneer
back to the flying boy in mountain air,

Vermont's child to go out, and while Keats sweat'
for hopeless inextricable lust, Henry's fate,
and Ethan Allen was a calling man,
all through the blind one's dream of the start,
when Day was killing Porter and had to part
lovers for ever, fancy if you can,

while the cardinals' guile to keep Aeneas out
was failing, while in some hearts Chinese doubt
inscrutably was growing, toward its end,
and a starved lion by a water-hole
clouded with gall, while Abelard was whole,
these grapes of stone were being proffered, friend.

Life, friends, is boring. We must not say so.
After all, the sky flashes, the great sea yearns,
we ourselves flash and yearn,
and moreover my mother told me as a boy
(repeatingly) 'Ever to confess you're bored
means you have no

Inner Resources.' I conclude now I have no
inner resources, because I am heavy bored.
Peoples bore me,
literature bores me, especially great literature,
Henry bores me, with his plights & gripes
as bad as achilles,

who loves people and valiant art, which bores me.
And the tranquil hills, & gin, look like a drag
and somehow a dog
has taken itself & its tail considerably away
into mountains or sea or sky, leaving
behind: me, wag.

Henry's pelt was put on sundry walls
where it did much resemble Henry and
them persons was delighted.
Especially his long & glowing tail
by all them was admired, and visitors.
They whistled: This is *it*!

Golden, whilst your frozen daiquiris
whir at midnight, gleams on you his fur
& silky & black.
Mission accomplished, pal.
My molten yellow & moonless bag,
drained, hangs at rest.

Collect in the cold depths barracuda. Ay,
in Sealdah Station some possessionless
children survive to die.
The Chinese communes hum. Two daiquiris
withdrew into a corner of the gorgeous room
and one told the other a lie.

I am the little man who smokes & smokes.
I am the girl who does know better but.
I am the king of the pool.
I am so wise I had my mouth sewn shut.
I am a government official & a goddamned fool.
I am a lady who takes jokes.

I am the enemy of the mind.
I am the auto salesman and lóve you.
I am a teenage cancer, with a plan.
I am the blackt-out man.
I am the woman powerful as a zoo.
I am two eyes screwed to my set, whose blind—

It is the Fourth of July.
Collect: while the dying man,
forgone by you creator, who forgives,
is gasping 'Thomas Jefferson still lives'
in vain, in vain, in vain.
I am Henry Pussy-cat! My whiskers fly.

The glories of the world struck me, made me aria, once.
—What happen then, Mr Bones?
if be you cares to say.
—Henry. Henry became interested in women's bodies,
his loins were & were the   scene of stupendous achievement.
Stupor. Knees, dear. Pray.

All the knobs & softnesses of, my God,
the ducking & trouble it swarm on Henry,
at one time.
—What happen then, Mr Bones?
you seems excited-like.
—Fell Henry back into   the original crime: art, rime

besides a sense of others, my God, my God,
and a jealousy for the honour (alive) of his country,
what can get more odd?
and discontent with the thriving gangs & pride.
—What happen then, Mr Bones?
—I had a most marvellous   piece of luck. I died.

The greens of the Ganges delta foliate.
Of heartless youth made late aware he pled:
Brownies, please come.
To Henry in his sparest times sometimes
the little people spread, & did friendly things;
then he was glad.

Pleased, at the worst, except with man, he shook
the brightest winter sun.
All the green lives
of the great delta, hours, hurt his migrant heart
in a safety of the steady 'plane. Please, please
come.

My friends, —he has been known to mourn, —I'll die;
live you, in the most wild, kindly, green
partly forgiving wood,
sort of forever and all those human sings
close not your better ears to, while good Spring
returns with a dance and a sigh.

29

There sat down, once, a thing on Henry's heart
só heavy, if he had a hundred years
& more, & weeping, sleepless, in all them time
Henry could not make good.
Starts again always in Henry's ears
the little cough somewhere, an odour, a chime.

And there is another thing he has in mind
like a grave Sienese face a thousand years
would fail to blur the still profiled reproach of. Ghastly,
with open eyes, he attends, blind.
All the bells say: too late. This is not for tears;
thinking.

But never did Henry, as he thought he did,
end anyone and hacks her body up
and hide the pieces, where they may be found.
He knows: he went over everyone, & nobody's missing.
Often he reckons, in the dawn, them up.
Nobody is ever missing.

Henry Hankovitch, con guítar,
did a short Zen pray,
on his tatami in a relaxed lotos
fixin his mind on nuffin, rose-blue breasts,
and gave his parnel one French kiss;
enslaving himself he withdrew from his blue

Florentine leather case an Egyptian black
& flickt a zippo.
Henry & Phoebe happy as cockroaches
in the world-kitchen woofed, with all away.
The international flame, like despair, rose
or like the foolish Paks or Sudanese

Henry Hankovitch, con guítar,
did a praying mantis pray
who even more obviously than the increasingly fanatical Americans
cannot govern themselves. Swedes don't exist,
Scandinavians in general do not exist,
take it from there.

34

My mother has your shotgun. One man, wide
in the mind, and tendoned like a grizzly, pried
to his trigger-digit, pal.
He should not have done that, but, I guess,
he didn't feel the best, Sister,—felt less
and more about less than us . . .?

Now—tell me, my love, *if* you recall
the dove light after dawn at the island and all—
here is the story, Jack:
he verbed for forty years, very enough,
& shot & buckt—and, baby, there was of
schist but small there (some).

Why should I tell a truth? when in the crack
of the dooming & emptying news I did hold back—
in the taxi too, sick—
silent—it's so I broke down here, in his mind
whose sire as mine one same way—I refuse,
hoping the guy go home.

36

The high ones die, die. They die. You look up and who's there?
—Easy, easy, Mr Bones. I is on your side.
I smell your grief.
—I sent my grief away. I cannot care
forever. With them all again & again I died
and cried, and I have to live.

—Now there *you* exaggerate, Sah. We hafta *die*.
That is our 'pointed task. Love & die.
—Yes; that makes sense.
But what makes sense between, then? What if I
roiling & babbling & braining, brood on why and
just sat on the fence?

—I doubts you did or do. De choice is lost.
—It's fool's gold. But I go in for that.
The boy & the bear
looked at each other. Man all is tossed
& lost with groin-wounds by the grand bulls, cat.
William Faulkner's where?

(Frost being still around.)

His malice was a pimple down his good
big face, with its sly eyes. I must be sorry
Mr Frost has left:
I like it so less I don't understood —
he couldn't hear or see well — all we sift —
but this is a *bad* story.

He had fine stories and was another man
in private; difficult, always. Courteous,
on the whole, in private.
He apologize to Henry, off & on,
for two blue slanders; which was good of him.
I don't know how he made it.

Quickly, off stage with all but kindness, now.
I can't say what I have in mind. Bless Frost,
any odd god around.
Gentle his shift, I decussate & command,
stoic deity. For a while here we possessed
an unusual man.

42

O journeyer, deaf in the mould, insane
with violent travel & death: consider me
in my cast, your first son.
Would you were I by now another one,
witted, legged? I see you before me plain
(I am skilled: I hear, I see)—

your honour was troubled: when you wondered—'No'.
I hear. I think I hear. Now full craze down
across our continent
all storms since you gave in, on my pup-tent.
I have of blast & counter to remercy you
for hurling me downtown.

We dream of honour, and we get along.
Fate winged me, in the person of a cab
and your stance on the sand.
Think it across, in freezing wind: withstand
my blistered wish: flop, there, to his blind song
who pick up the tab.

45

He stared at ruin. Ruin stared straight back.
He thought they was old friends. He felt on the stair
where her papa found them bare
they became familiar. When the papers were lost
rich with pals' secrets, he thought he had the knack
of ruin. Their paths crossed

and once they crossed in jail; they crossed in bed;
and over an unsigned letter their eyes met,
and in an Asian city
directionless & lurchy at two & three,
or trembling to a telephone's fresh threat,
and when some wired his head

to reach a wrong opinion, 'Epileptic'.
But he noted now that: they were not old friends.
He did not know this one.
This one was a stranger, come to make amends
for all the imposters, and to make it stick.
Henry nodded, un-.

I am, outside. Incredible panic rules.
People are blowing and beating each other without mercy.
Drinks are boiling. Iced
drinks are boiling. The worse anyone feels, the worse
treated he is. Fools elect fools.
A harmless man at an intersection said, under his breath: 'Christ!'

That word, so spoken, affected the vision
of, when they trod to work next day, shopkeepers
who went & were fitted for glasses.
Enjoyed they then an appearance of love & law.
Millenia whift & waft—one, one—er, er . . .
Their glasses were taken from them, & they saw.

Man has undertaken the top job of all,
son fin. Good luck.
I myself walked at the funeral of tenderness.
Followed other deaths. Among the last,
like the memory of a lovely fuck,
was: *Do, ut des.*

47 April Fool's Day, or, St Mary of Egypt

— Thass a funny title, Mr Bones.
— When down she saw her feet, sweet fish, on the threshold,
she considered her fair shoulders
and all them hundreds who have held them, all
the more who to her mime thickened & maled
from the supple stage,

and seeing her feet, in a visit, side by side
paused on the sill of The Tomb, she shrank: 'No.
They are not worthy,
fondled by many' and rushed from The Crucified
back through her followers out of the city ho
across the suburbs, plucky

to dare my desert in her late daylight
of animals and sands. She fall prone.
Only wind whistled.
And forty-seven years went by like Einstein.
We celebrate her feast with our caps on,
whom God has not visited.

48

He yelled at me in Greek,
my God! — It's not his language
and I'm no good at—his is Aramaic,
was—I am a monoglot of English
(American version) and, say pieces from
a baker's dozen others; where's the bread?

but rising in the Second Gospel, pal:
The seed goes down, god dies,
a rising happens,
some crust, and then occurs   an eating. He said so,
a Greek idea,
troublesome to imaginary Jews,

like bitter Henry, full of the death of love,
Cawdor-uneasy, disambitious, mourning
the whole implausible necessary thing.
He dropped his voice & sybilled of
the death of the death of love.
I óught to get going.

Old Pussy-cat if he won't eat, he don't
feel good into his tum', old Pussy-cat.
He *wants* to have eaten.
Tremor, heaves, he sweaterings. He can't.
A dizzy swims of where is Henry at;
. . . somewhere streng verboten.

How come he sleeps & sleeps and sleeps, waking like death:
locate the restorations of which we hear
as of profound sleep.
From daylight he got maintrackt, from friends' breath,
wishes, his hopings. Dreams make crawl with fear
Henry but not get up.

The course his mind his body steer, poor Pussy-cat,
in weakness & disorder, will see him down
whiskers & tail.
'Wastethrift': Oh one of cunning wives know that
he hoardy-squander, where is nor downtown
neither suburba. Braille.

51

Our wounds to time, from all the other times,
sea-times slow, the times of galaxies
fleeing, the dwarfs' dead times,
lessen so little that if here in his crude rimes
Henry them mentions, do not hold it, please,
for a putting of man down.

Ol' Marster, being bound you do your best
versus we coons, spare now a cagey John
a whilom bits that whip:
who'll tell your fortune, when you have confessed
whose & whose woundings — against the innocent stars
& remorseless seas —

— Are you radioactive, pal? — Pal, radioactive.
— Has you the night sweats & the day sweats, pal?
— Pal, I do.
— Did your gal leave you? — What do *you* think, pal?
— Is that thing on the front of your head what it seems to be, pal?
— Yes, pal.

Bright-eyed & bushy-tailed woke not Henry up.
Bright though upon his workshop shone a vise
central, moved in
while he was doing time down hospital
and growing wise.
He gave it the worst look he had left.

Alone. They all abandoned   Henry—wonder! all,
when most he—under the sun.
That was all right.
He can't work well with it here, or think.
A bilocation, yellow like catastrophe.
The name of this was freedom.

Will Henry again ever be on the lookout for women & milk,
honour & love again,
have a buck or three?
He felt like shrieking but he shuddered as
(spring mist, warm, rain) an handful with quietness
vanisht & the thing took hold.

53

He lay in the middle of the world, and twitcht.
More Sparine for Pelides,
human (half) & down here as he is,
with probably insulting mail to open
and certainly unworthy words to hear
and his unforgivable memory.

—I seldom *go* to *films*. They are too exciting,
said the Honourable Possum.
—It takes me so long to read the 'paper,
said to me one day a novelist hot as a firecracker,
because I have to identify myself with everyone in it,
including the corpses, pal.'

Kierkegaard wanted a society, to refuse to read 'papers,
and that was not, friends, his worst idea.
Tiny Hardy, toward the end, refused to say *anything*,
a programme adopted early on by long Housman,
and Gottfried Benn
said:— We are using our own skins for wallpaper and we cannot win.

54

'NO VISITORS' I thumb the roller to
and leans against the door.
Comfortable in my horseblanket
I prop on the costly bed & dream of my wife,
my first wife,
and my second wife & my son.

Insulting, they put guardrails up,
as if it were a crib!
I growl at the head nurse; we compose on one.
I have been operating from *nothing*,
like a dog after its tail
more slowly, losing altitude.

Nitid. They are shooting me full of sings.
I give no rules. Write as short as you can,
in order, of what matters.
I think of my beloved poet
Issa & his father who
sat down on the grass and took leave of each other.

55

Peter's not friendly. He gives me sideways looks.
The architecture is far from reassuring.
I feel uneasy.
A pity,—the interview began so well:
I mentioned fiendish things, he waved them away
and sloshed out a martini

strangely needed. We spoke of indifferent matters—
God's health, the vague hell of the Congo,
John's energy,
anti-matter matter. I felt fine.
Then a change came backward. A chill fell.
Talk slackened,

died, and he began to give me sideways looks.
'Christ,' I thought 'what now?' and would have askt for another
but didn't dare.
I feel my application   failing. It's growing dark,
some other sound is overcoming. His last words are:
'We betrayed me.'

'All virtues enter into this world:')
A Buddhist, doused in the street, serenely burned.
The Secretary of State for War,
winking it over, screwed a redhaired whore.
Monsignor Capovilla mourned. What a week.   ·
A journalism doggy took a leak

against absconding coon ('but take one virtue,
without which a man can hardly hold his own')
the sun in the willow
shivers itself & shakes itself green-yellow
(Abba Pimen groaned, over the telephone,
when asked what that was:)

How feel a fellow then when he arrive
in fame but lost? but affable, top-shelf.
Quelle sad semaine.
He hardly know his selving. ('that a man')
Henry grew hot, got laid, felt bad, survived
('should always reproach himself'.

I don't operate often. When I do,
persons take note.
Nurses look amazed. They pale.
The patient is brought back to life, or so.
The reason I don't do this more (I quote)
is: I have a living to fail—

because of my wife & son—to keep from earning.
—Mr Bones, I sees that.
They for these operations thanks you, what?
not pays you. —Right.
You have seldom been so understanding.
Now there is further a difficulty with the light:

I am obliged to perform in complete darkness
operations of great delicacy
on my self.
—Mr Bones, you terrifies me.
No wonder they don't pay you. Will you die?
—My
                    friend, I succeeded. Later.

Love her he doesn't but the thought he puts
into that young woman
would launch a national product
complete with TV spots & skywriting
outlets in Bonn & Tokyo
I mean it

Let it be known that nine words have not passed
between herself and Henry;
looks, smiles.
God help Henry, who deserves it all
every least part of that infernal & unconscious
woman, and the pain.

I feel as if, unique, she . . . Biddable?
Fates, conspire.
— Mr Bones, *please*.
— Vouchsafe me, Sleepless One,
a personal experience of the body of Mrs Boogry
before I pass from lust!

Spellbound held subtle Henry all his four
hearers in the racket of the market
with ancient signs, infamous characters,
new rhythms. On the steps he was beloved,
hours a day, by all his four, or more,
depending. And they paid him.

It was not, so, like no one listening
but critics famed & Henry's pals or other
tellers at all
chiefly in another country. No.
He by the heart & brains & tail, because
of their love for it, had them.

Junk he said to all them open-mouthed.
Weather wóuld govern. When the monsoon spread
its floods, few came, two.
Came a day when none, though he began
in his accustomed way on the filthy steps
in a crash of waters, came.

Henry hates the world. What the world to Henry
did will not bear thought.
Feeling no pain,
Henry stabbed his arm and wrote a letter
explaining how bad it had been
in this world.

Old yellow, in a gown
might have made a difference, 'these lower beauties',
and chartreuse could have mattered

'Kyoto, Toledo,
Benares — the holy cities —
and Cambridge shimmering do not make up
for, well, the horror of unlove,
nor south from Paris driving in the Spring
to Siena and on . . .'

Pulling together Henry, somber Henry
woofed at things.
Spry disappointments of men
and vicing adorable children
miserable women, Henry mastered, Henry
tasting all the secret bits of life.

Turning it over, considering, like a madman
Henry put forth a book.
No harm resulted from this.
Neither the menstruating   stars (nor man) was moved
at once.
Bare dogs drew closer for a second look

and performed their friendly operations there.
Refreshed, the bark rejoiced.
Seasons went and came.
Leaves fell, but only a few.
Something remarkable about this
unshedding bulky bole-proud blue-green moist

thing made by savage & thoughtful
surviving Henry
began to strike the passers from despair
so that sore on their shoulders old men hoisted
six-foot sons and polished women called
small girls to dream awhile toward the flashing & bursting tree!

Nothin very bad happen to me lately.
How you explain that?—I explain that, Mr Bones,
terms o' your bafflin odd sobriety.
Sober as man can get, no girls, no telephones,
what could happen bad to Mr Bones?
— *If* life is a handkerchief sandwich,

in a modesty of death I join my father
who dared so long agone leave me.
A bullet on a concrete stoop
close by a smothering southern sea
spreadeagled on an island, by my knee.
— You is from hunger, Mr Bones,

I offers you this handkerchief, now set
your left foot by my right foot,
shoulder to shoulder, all that jazz,
arm in arm, by the beautiful sea,
hum a little, Mr Bones.
—I saw nobody coming, so I went instead.

Seedy Henry rose up shy in de world
& shaved & swung his barbells, duded Henry up
and p.a.'d poor thousands of persons on topics of grand
moment to Henry, ah to those less & none.
Wif a book of his in either hand
he is stript down to move on.

—Come away, Mr Bones.

—Henry is tired of the winter,
& haircuts, & a squeamish comfy   ruin-prone proud national
        mind,   & Spring (in the city so called).
Henry likes Fall.
Hé would be prepared to líve in a world of Fáll
for ever, impenitent Henry.
But the snows and summers grieve & dream;

thése fierce & airy occupations, and love,
raved away so many of Henry's years
it is a wonder that, with in each hand
one of his own mad books and all,
ancient fires for eyes, his head full
& his heart full, he's making ready to move on.

NO INTERESTING PROJECT CAN BE EMBARKED ON WITHOUT FEAR. I SHALL BE
SCARED TO DEATH HALF THE TIME.
Sir Francis Chichester in Sydney

FOR MY PART I AM ALWAYS FRIGHTENED, AND VERY MUCH SO. I FEAR THE
FUTURE OF ALL ENGAGEMENTS.
Gordon in Khartoum

I AM PICKT UP AND SORTED TO A PIP. MY IMAGINATION IS A MONASTERY
AND I AM ITS MONK.
Keats to Shelley

HE WENT AWAY AND NEVER SAID GOODBYE.
I COULD READ HIS LETTERS BUT I SURE CAN'T READ HIS MIND.
I THOUGHT HE'S LOVIN ME BUT HE WAS LEAVIN ALL THE TIME.
NOW I KNOW THAT MY TRUE LOVE WAS BLIND.
Victoria Spivey?

Darkened his eye, his wild smile disappeared,
inapprehensible his studies grew,
nourished he less & less
his subject body with good food & rest,
something bizarre about Henry, slowly sheared
off, unlike you & you,

smaller & smaller, till in question stood
his eyeteeth and one block of memories
These were enough for him
implying commands from upstairs & from down,
Walt's 'orbic flex,' triads of Hegel would
incorporate, if you please,

into the know-how of the American bard
embarrassed Henry heard himself a-being,
and the younger Stephen Crane
of a powerful memory, of pain,
these stood the ancestors, relaxed & hard,
whilst Henry's parts were fleeing.

Plop, plop. The lobster toppled in the pot.
fulfilling, dislike man, his destiny,
glowing fire-red,
succulent, and on the whole becoming what
man wants. I crack my final claw singly,
wind up the grave, & to bed.

—Sound good, Mr Bones. I wish I had me some.
(I spose you got a lessen up your slave.)
—O no no no.
Sole I remember; where no lobster swine,—
pots hots or cold is none. With you I grieve
lightly, and I have no lesson.

Bodies are relishy, they say. Here's mine,
was. What ever happened to Political Economy,
leaving me here?
Is a rare—in my opinion—responsibility.
The military establishments perpetuate themselves forever.
Have a bite, for a sign.

The conclusion is growing . . . I feel sure, my lord,
this august court will entertain the plea
Not Guilty by reason of death.
I can say no more except that for the record
I add that all the crimes since all the times he
died will be due to the breath

of unknown others, sweating in their guilt
while my client Henry's brow of stainless steel
rests free, as well it may,
of all such turbulence, whereof not built
Henry lies clear as any onion-peel
in any sandwich, say.

He spiced us: there, my lord, the wicked fault
lodges: we judged him when we did not know
and we did judge him wrong,
lying incapable of crime save salt
preservative in cases here below
adduced. Not to prolong

these hearings endlessly, friends, word is had
Henry may be returning to our life
adult & difficult.
There exist rumours that remote & sad
and quite beyond the knowledge of his wife
to the foothills of the cult

will come in silence this distinguished one
essaying once again the lower slopes
in triumph, keeping up our hopes,
and heading not for the highest we have done
but enigmatic faces, unsurveyed,
calm as a forest glade

for him. I only speak of what I hear
and I have said too much. He may be there
or he may groan in hospital
resuming, as the fates decree, our lot.
I would not interrupt him in whatever, in what
he's bracing him to at all.

In slack times visit I the violent dead
and pick their awful brains. Most seem to feel
nothing is secret more
to my disdain I find, when we who fled
cherish the knowings of both worlds, conceal
more, beat on the floor,

where Bhain is stagnant, dear of Henry's friends,
yellow with cancer, paper-thin, & bent
even in the hospital bed
racked with high hope, on whom death lay hands
in weeks, or Yeats in the London spring half-spent,
only the grand gift in his head

going for him, a seated ruin of a man
courteous to a junior, like one of the boarders,
or Dylan, with more to say
now there's no hurry, and we're all a clan.
You'd think off here one would be free from orders.
I didn't hear a single   word. I obeyed.

In a blue series towards his sleepy eyes
they slid like wonder, women tall & small,
of every shape & size,
in many languages to lisp 'We do'
to Henry almost waking. What is the night at all,
his closed eyes beckon you.

In the Marriage of the Dead, a new routine,
he gasped his crowded vows past lids shut tight
and a-many rings fumbled on.
His coffin like Grand Central to the brim
filled up & emptied with the lapse of light.
Which one will waken him?

O she must startle like a fallen gown,
content with speech like an old sacrament
in deaf ears lying down,
blazing through darkness till he feels the cold
 & blindness of his hopeless tenement
while his black arms unfold.

In the night-reaches dreamed he of better graces,
of liberations, and beloved faces,
such as now ere dawn he sings.
It would not be easy, accustomed to these things,
to give up the old world, but he could try;
let it all rest, have a good cry.

Let Randall rest, whom your self-torturing
cannot restore one instant's good to, rest:
he's left us now.
The panic died and in the panic's dying
so did my old friend. I am headed west
also, also, somehow.

In the chambers of the end we'll meet again
I will say Randall, he'll say Pussycat
and all will be as before
whenas we sought, among the beloved faces,
eminence and were dissatisfied with that
and needed more.

Noises from underground made gibber some,
others collected & dug Henry up
saying 'You *are* a sight.'
Chilly, he muttered for a double rum
waving the mikes away, putting a stop
to rumours, pushing his fright

off with the now accumulated taxes
accustomed in his way to solitude
and no bills.
Wives came forward, claiming a new Axis,
fearful for their insurance, though, now, glued
to disencumbered Henry's many ills.

A fortnight later, sense a single man
upon the trampled scene at 2 a.m.
insomnia-plagued, with a shovel
digging like mad, Lazarus with a plan
to get his own back, a plan, a stratagem
no newsman will unravel.

Something black somewhere   in the vistas of his heart.

Tulips from Tates teazed Henry in the mood
to be a tulip and desire no more
but water, but light, but air.
Yet his nerves rattled blackly, unsubdued,
 & suffocation called, dream-whiskey'd pour
sirening. Rosy there

too fly my Phil & Ellen roses, pal.
Flesh-coloured men & women come & punt
under my windows. I rave
or grunt against it, from a flowerless land.
For timeless hours wind most, or not at all. I wind
my clock before I shave.

Soon it will fall dark. Soon you'll see stars
you fevered after, child, man, & did nothing, —
compass live to the pencil-torch!
As still as his cadaver, Henry mars
this surface of an earth or other, feet south
eyes bleared west, waking to march.

99   Temples

He does not live here but it *is* the god.
A priest tools in atop his motorbike.
You do not enter.
He does not enter.
Us the landscape circles hard abroad,
sunned, stone. Like calls, too low, to like.
One submachine-gun cleared the Durga Temple.

It is very dark here in this groping forth

                Gulp rhubarb for a guilty heart,
rhubarb for a free, if the world's sway
waives customs anywhere that far

Look on, without pure dismay.
Unable to account for itself.

The slave-girl folded her fan & turned on my air-conditioner.
The lemonade-machine made lemonade.
I made love, lolled,
my roundel lowered. I ache less. I purr.
—Mr Bones, you too advancer with your song,
muching of which are wrong.

Sixteen below. Our cars like stranded hulls
litter all day our little Avenue.
It *was* 28 below.
No one goes anywhere. Fabulous calls
to duty clank. Icy dungeons, though,
have much to mention to you.

At Harvard & Yale must Pussy-cat be heard
in the dead of winter when we must be sad
and feel by the weather had.
Chrysanthemums crest, far away, in the Emperor's garden
and, whenever we are, we must beg always pardon
Pardon was the word.

Pardon was the only word, in ferocious cold
like Asiatic prisons, where we live
and strive and strive to forgive.
Melted my honey, summers ago. I told
her true & summer things. She leaned an ear
in my direction, here.

He wondered: Do I love? all this applause,
young beauties sitting at my feet & all,
and all.
It tires me out, he pondered: I'm tempted to break laws
and love myself, or the stupid questions asked me
move me to homicide —

so many beauties, one on either side,
the wall's behind me, into which I crawl
out of my repeating voice —
the mike folds down, the foolish askers fall
over themselves in an audience of ashes
and Henry returns to rejoice

in dark & still, and one sole beauty only
who never walked near Henry while the mob
was at him like a club:
she saw through things, she saw that he was lonely
and waited while he hid behind the wall
and all.

It was only a small dream of the Golden World,
now you trot off to bed. I'll turn the machine off,
you've danced & trickt us enough.
Unintelligible whines & imprecations, hurled
from the second floor, fail to impress your mother
and I am the only other

and I say go to bed! We'll meet tomorrow,
acres of threats dissolve into a smile,
you'll be the *Little* Baby
again, while I pursue my path of sorrow
& bodies, bodies, to be carried a mile
& dropt. Maybe

if frozen slush will represent the soul
which is to represented in the hereafter
I ask for a decree
dooming my bitter enemies to laughter
advanced against them. If the dream was small
it was my dream also, Henry's.

The animal moment, when   he sorted out her tail
in a rump session with the vivid hostess
whose guests had finally gone,
was stronger, though so limited, though failed
all normal impulse before her interdiction, yes,
and Henry gave in.

I'd like to have your baby, but, she moaned,
I'm married. Henry muttered to himself
So am I and was glad
to keep chaste. If this lady he had had
scarcely could he have have ever forgiven himself
and how would he have atoned?

—Mr Bones, you strong on moral these days, hey?
It's good to be faithful but it ain't natural,
as you knows.
—I knew what I knew when I knew when I was astray,
all those bright painful years, forgiving all
but when Henry & his wives came to blows.

Also I love him: me he's done no wrong
for going on forty years—forgiveness time—
I touch now his despair,
he felt as bad as Whitman on his tower
but he did not swim out with me or my brother
as he threatened—

a powerful swimmer, to   take one of us along
as company in the defeat sublime,
freezing my helpless mother:
he only, very early in the morning,
rose with his gun and went outdoors by my window
and did what was needed.

I cannot read that wretched mind, so strong
& so undone. I've always tried. I—I'm
trying to forgive
whose frantic passage, when he could not live
an instant longer, in the summer dawn
left Henry to live on.

These lovely motions of the air, the breeze,
tell me I'm not in hell, though round me the dead
lie in their limp postures
dramatizing the dreadful word *instead*
for lively Henry, fit for debaucheries
and bird-of-paradise vestures

only his heart is elsewhere, down with them
 & down with Delmore specially, the new ghost
haunting Henry most:
though fierce the claims of others, coimedela crime
came the Hebrew spectre, on a note of woe
and Join me O.

'Down with them all!' Henry suddenly cried.
Their deaths were theirs. I wait on for my own,
I dare say it won't be long.
I have tried to be them, god knows I have tried,
but they are past it all, I have not done,
which brings me to the end of this song.

Henry's mind grew blacker the more he thought.
He looked onto the world like the act of an aged whore.
Delmore, Delmore.
He flung to pieces and they hit the floor.
Nothing was true but what Marcus Aurelius taught,
'All that is foul smell & blood in a bag.'

He lookt on the world like the leavings of a hag.
Almost his love died from him, any more.
His mother & William
were vivid in the same mail Delmore died.
The world is lunatic. This is the last ride.
Delmore, Delmore.

High in the summer branches the poet sang.
His throat ached, and he could sing no more.
All ears closed
across the heights where Delmore & Gertrude sprang
so long ago, in the goodness of which it was composed
Delmore, Delmore!

I'm cross with god who has wrecked this generation.
First he seized Ted, then Richard, Randall, and now Delmore.
In between he gorged on Sylvia Plath.
That was a first rate haul. He left alive
fools I could number like a kitchen knife
but Lowell he did not touch.

Somewhere the enterprise continues, not—
yellow the sun lies on the baby's blouse—
in Henry's staggered thought.
I suppose the word would be, we must submit.
Later.
I hang, and I will not be part of it.

A friend of Henry's contrasted God's career
with Mozart's, leaving Henry with nothing to say
but praise for a word so apt.
We suffer on, a day, a day, a day.
And never again can come, like a man slapped,
news like this

Flagrant his young male beauty, thick his mind
with lore and passionate, white his devotion
to Gertrude only,
but even that marriage fell on days were lonely
and ended, and the trouble with friends got into motion,
when Delmore undermined

his closest loves with merciless suspicion:
Dwight cheated him out of a house, Saul withheld money,
and then to cap it all,
Henry was not here in '57
during his troubles (Henry was in Asia),
accusations to appall

the Loyal forever, but the demands increast:
as I said to my house in Providence
at 8 a.m. in a Cambridge taxi,
which he had wait, later he telephoned
at midnight from New York, to bring my family
to New York, leaving my job.

All your bills will be paid, he added, tense.

I can't get him out of my mind, out of my mind,
Hé was out of his own mind for years,
in police stations & Bellevue.
He drove up to my house in Providence
ho ho at 8 a.m. in a Cambridge taxi
and told it to wait.

He walked my living-room, & did not want breakfast
or even coffee, or even even a drink.
He paced, I'd say Sit down,
it makes me nervous, for a moment he'd sit down,
then pace. After an hour or so *I* had a drink.
He took it back to Cambridge,

we never learnt why he came, or what he wanted.
His mission was obscure. His mission was real,
but obscure.
I remember his electrical insight as the young man,
his wit & passion, gift, the whole young man
alive with surplus love.

I give in. I must not leave   the scene of this same death
as most of me strains to.
There are all the problems to be sorted out,
the fate of the soul, what it was all about
during its being, and whether he was drunk
at 4 a.m. on the wrong floor too

fighting for air, tearing his sorry clothes
with his visions dying O and O I mourn
again this complex death
Almost my oldest friend should never have been born
to this terrible end, out of which what grows
but an unshaven, dissheveled *corpse*?

The spirit & the joy, in memory
live of him on, the young will read his young verse
for as long as such things go:
why then do I despair, miserable Henry
who *knew* him all so long, for better & worse
and nearly would follow him below.

I have strained everything except my ears,
he marvelled to himself: and they're too dull—
owing to one childhood illness—
outward, for strain; inward, too smooth & fierce
for painful strain as back at the onset, yes
when Henry keen & viable

began to poke his head from Venus' foam
toward the grand shore, where all them ears would be
if any.
Thus his art started. Thus he ran from home
toward home, forsaking too withal his mother
in the almost unbearable smother.

He strained his eyes, his brain, his nervous system,
for a beginning; cracked an ankle & arm;
it cannot well be denied
that nearly all the rest of him came to harm
too . . . Only his ears sat with his theme
in the splices of his pride.

and God has many other surprises, like
when the man you fear most in the world marries your mother
and chilling other,
men from far tribes armed in the dark, the dike-
hole, the sudden gash of an old friend's betrayal,
words out that leave one pale,

milk & honey in the old house, mouth gone bad,
the caress that felt for all the world like a blow,
screams of fear eyeless, wide-eyed loss,
hellish vaudeville turns, promises had
 & promises forgotten here below,
the final wound of the Cross.

I have a story to tell you which is the worst
story to tell that ever once I heard.
What thickens my tongue?
and has me by the throat? I gasp accursed
even for the thought of uttering that word.
I pass to the next Song:

Go, ill-sped book, and whisper to her or
storm out the message for her only ear
that she is beautiful.
Mention sunsets, be not silent of her eyes
and mouth and other prospects, praise her size,
say her figure is full.

Say her small figure is heavenly & full,
so as stunned Henry yatters like a fool
& maketh little sense.
Say she is soft in speech, stately in walking,
modest at gatherings, and in every thing
declare her excellence.

Forget not, when the rest is wholly done
and all her splendours opened one by one
to add that she likes Henry,
for reasons unknown, and fate has bound them fast
one to another in linkages that last
and that are fair to see.

Your face broods from my table, Suicide.
Your force came on like a torrent toward the end
of agony and wrath.
You were christened in the beginning Sylvia Plath
and changed that name for Mrs Hughes and bred
and went on round the bend

till the oven seemed the proper place for you.
I brood upon your face, the geography of grief,
hooded, till I allow
again your resignation from us now
though the screams of orphaned children fix me anew.
Your torment here was brief,

long falls your exit all repeatingly,
a poor exemplum, one more suicide
to stack upon the others
till stricken Henry with his sisters & brothers
suddenly gone pauses to wonder why he
alone breasts the wronging tide.

Somebody once pronounced upon one Path.
What rhythm shall we use for Richard's death,
the dearer of the dear,
my older friend of three blackt out on me
I am heartbroken — open-heart surgery — see!
but I am not full of fear.

Richard is quiet who talked on so well:
I fill with fear: I agree: all this is hell
Where will he lie?
In a tantrum of horror & blocking where will he be?
With Helen, whom he softened — see! see! see!
But not nearby.

Which search for Richard will not soon be done.
I blow on the live coal. I would be one,
another one.
Surely the galaxy will scratch my itch
Augustinian, like the night-wind witch
and I will love that touch.

Failed as a makar, nailed as scholar, failed
as a father & a man, hailed for a lover,
Henry slumped down, pored it over.
We c-can't win here, he stammered to himself.
With his friend Phil and also his friend Ralph
he mourned across or he wailed.

His friend Boyd waited, all behind the nurses,
the simple nurses pretty as you will,
and emerged, and gave.
He was as ill as well one can be, ill.
When he could read he studied for gravestones
the *Geographic*, with curses.

And neither did his friend Boyd haul him up
entirely, nor did Ralph & Phil succeed
dispersing his gross fears.
He leaned on Heaven; no. Black would he bleed
to tests. Their EEG for months, for years,
went mad. So did not he.

There is a swivelly grace that's up from grace
I both remember & know. Into your face
for summers now — for three —
I have been looking, and for winters O
and never at any time have you resembled snow.
And at the ceremony

after His Honor swivelled us a judge
my best friend stood in tears, at both his age
and undeclining mine.
In E(e)rie Plaza then we kept on house
and months O soon we saw that pointy-nose
was destined to combine

her blood with Henry's in a little thing.
If all went well. It all went better, mingling,
and Little sprang out.
The parking-lot tilted & made a dance,
ditching Jesuits. The sun gave it a glance
and went about & about.

I stalk my mirror down this corridor
my pieces litter. Oklahoma, sore
from my great loss leaves me.
We pool our knowless in my seminar,
question all comers that they may not jar
their intrepidity

before the Awenger rises in the corpse's way
as inconvenient as the bloodscoot sway
of them Aztecs' real priests.
All my pieces kneel and we all scream:
History's Two-legs was a heartless dream,
reality is

& reskinned knuckles & forgiveness & toys
unbreakable & thunder that excites & annoys
but's powerless to harm.
Reality's the growing again of the right arm
(which so we missed in our misleading days)
& the popping back in of eyes.

Hung by a thread more moments instant Henry's mind
super-subtle, which he knew blunt & empty & incurious
but when he compared it with his fellows'
finding it keen & full, he didn't know what to think
apart from typewriters & print & ink.
On the philosophical side

plus religious, he lay at a loss.
Mostly he knew the ones he would not follow
into their burning systems
or polar systems, Wittgenstein being boss,
Augustine general manager. A universal hollow
most of the other seems;

so Henry in twilight is on his own:
marrying, childing, slogging, shelling taxes,
pondering, making.
It's rained all day. His wife has been away
with genuine difficulty he fought madness
whose breast came close to breaking.

It's wonderful the way cats bound about,
it's wonderful how men are not found out
so far.
It's miserable how many   miserable are
over the spread world at this tick of time.
These mysteries that I'm

rehearsing in the dark did brighter minds
much bother through them ages, whom who finds
guilty for failure?
Up all we rose with dawn, springy for pride,
trying all morning. Dazzled, I subside
at noon, noon be my gaoler

and afternoon the deepening of the task
poor Henry set himself long since to ask :
Why? Who? When?
—I don know, Mr Bones. You asks too much
of such as you & me & we & such
fast cats, worse men.

Misunderstanding. Misunderstanding, misunderstanding.
Are we stationed here among another thing?
Sometimes I wonder.
After the lightning, this afternoon, came thunder:
the natural world makes sense: cats hate water
and love fish.

Fish, plankton, bats' radar, the sense of fish
who glide up the coast of South America
and head for Gibraltar.
How do they know it's there? We call this *instinct*
by which we dream we know what instinct is,
like misunderstanding.

I was soft on a green girl once and we smiled across
and married, childed. Never did we truly take in
one burning wing.
Henry flounders. What is the name of that fish?
So better organized than we are oh.
Sing to me that name, enchanter, sing!

Am I a bad man? Am I a good man?
—Hard to say, Brother Bones. Maybe you both,
like most of we.
—The evidence is difficult to structure towards deliberate evil.
But what of the rest? Does it wax for wrath
in its infinite complexity?

She left without a word, for Ecuador.
I would have liked to discuss more with her this thing
through the terrible nights.
She was than Henry wiser, being younger or
a woman. She brought me Sanka and violent drugs
which were yet wholly inadequate.

My doctor doubles them daily. Am I a bad one—
I'm thinking of them fires & their perplexness—
or may a niche be found
in nothingness for completely exhausted Henry?
But it comes useless to canvass this alone,
out of her eyes and sound.

Leaving behind the country of the dead
where he must then return & die himself
he set his tired face due East
where the sun rushes up the North Atlantic
and where had paused a little the war for bread
 & the war for status had ceased

forever, and he took with him five books,
a Whitman & a Purgatorio,
a one-volume dictionary,
an Oxford Bible with all its bays & nooks
 & bafflements long familiar to Henry
 & one other new book-O.

If ever he had crafted in the past—
but only if—he swore now to craft better
which lay in the Hands above.
He said: I'll work on slow, O slow & fast,
if a letter comes I will answer that letter
 & my whole year will be tense with love.

Decision taken, Henry'll be back abroad,
from where things look more inter'sting, where things
American are seen
without America's perpetual self-laud
as if everything in America had wings,
the world else a crawling scene,

the world else peripheral. Now good London crimes,
Irish & Spanish sports, Japanese disasters
will heave him free to think.
He'll still have a bad ol' *Time* each week, & *The Times*
to clue him in to the actions of his masters.
He bought a lot of ink,

having much to say, masterless after all, & gay
with probability, time being on his side,
the large work largely done,
over the years, the prizes won,
we work now for ourself alone, away
even from pal & wife, in ways not to be denied.

Richard & Randall, & one who never did,
two who will never cross this sea again,
 & Delmore,
filled his pitted mind as the ship forged on
I hear the three freaks in their different notes
discussing more & more

our meaning to the Old World, theirs to us
which much we pondered in our younger years
and then coughed & sang
the new forms in which ancient thought appears
the altering bodies of the labile souls,
foes fang on fang.

The lovely friends, and friends the friends of friends,
pursuing insights to their journeys' ends
subtle & steadfast:
the wind blows hard from our past into our future
and we are that wind, except that the wind's nature
was not to last.

Shrouded the great stars, the great boat moves on.
A minimum of tremor in the bar.
Today was Children's Day
 & the Little Twiss prinked out ah as a bunny
won or did not win—I forget—second prize:
I forget to say.

I forget the great ship steaming thro' the dark
I forget the souls *so* eager for their pain.
Two have just dropt in,
grand ships' officers, large heads & gold braid,
the authority of the bartender is dwarfed
I forget all the old

I seem to be Henry then at twenty-one
steaming the sea again   in another British boat
again, half mad with hope:
with my loved Basque friend I stroll the topmost deck
high in the windy night, in love with life
which has produced this wreck.

In neighbourhoods evil of noise, he deployed, Henry,
stance unheroic. Say yes without offending.
In our career here
good will we too with ill. Wrinkle a grin.
The place is not so bad, considering
the alternative with real fear.

Being dead, I mean. 'Well it is a long rest'
to himself said Mr Bloom. But is it that now?
As one Hungarian
Jew to another, I have seen grins that test
our patience, pal. Things are getting out
of hand, gaffered another one.

Blundering, faltering, uphill all the way
& icy. O say yes without offending.
His heart, a mud-puddle, sang.
'Serve, Serve' it sang, and it sang that all day.
New tasks will craze you in your happy ending.
Let go without a pang.

It is, after all her! & in the late afternoon
of the last day! & she is even more delightful
than longing Henry expected:
Parisienne, bi-lingual, teaches English,
at 27 unmarried, for she has not found
anyone 'not ordinary':

(another couple in the Club have come to terms)
on this last day she is more beautiful high-coloured
even than Henry's wife
who is pale, pale & beautiful: Yvette's ankles
are slim as the thought of various poets I could mention
& she tilts her head proudly.

'Twould not be possible for her to lose her dignity,
I notice this at dusk in a rising sea,
such an excellent lady
I will have more to say at a later time
with my whole cracked heart, in prose or rhyme
of this lady of the northern sea.

Shifted his mind & was once more full of the great Dean
with his oddities about money & his enigmatic ladies,
the giant presences
chained to St Patrick's, tumultuous, serene,
their mighty stint done, larger in stone than life,
larger than Henry's belief

who now returns at fifty, conflict-scarred,
to see how they are doing: why, they are doing
just what thirty years ago
he thought they were doing, and it is not hard,
neither in doubt or trouble, neither gaining nor losing,
just being the same O.

His frantic huge mind left him long before the end,
he wandered mad through the apartments but once was seen
to pause by a shelf & look
at a copy of the *Tale of a Tub*: he took it down
& was heard to mutter 'What a genius was mine
when I wrote down that book.'

Cold & golden lay the high heroine
in a wilderness of bears. The forest tramped.
Henry was not at ease.
Intrusions had certainly been made on his dignities,
to his fury. Looking around, he felt cramped.
He said: This place is *theirs*,

I'll remove elsewhere, I will not live here
among my thugs. Lo, and he went away
to Dublin's fair city.
There he met at once two ladies dear
with problems, problems. Henry could not say
like their parish priest 'Pray'.

He immersed himself in their disabled fates
the catafalque above all for instance T—'s
and others' bound to come
The White House invitation came today,
three weeks after the reception, hey,
Henry not being at home.

Like the sunburst up the white breast of a black-footed penguin
amid infinite quantities of gin
Henry perceived his subject.
It came nearer, like a guilty bystander,
stood close, leaving no room to ponder,
Mickey Mouse & The Tiger on the table.

Leaving the ends aft open, touch the means,
whereby we ripen. Touch by all means the means
whereby we come to life,
enduring the manner for the matter, ay
I sing quickly, offered Henry, I
sing more quickly.

I sing with infinite slowness finite pain
I have reached into the corner of my brain
to have it out.
I sat by fires when I was young, & now
I'm not I sit by fires again, although
I do it more slowly.

I have moved to Dublin to have it out with you,
majestic Shade, You whom I read so well
so many years ago,
did I read your lesson right? did I see through
your phases to the real? your heaven, your hell
did I enquire properly into?

For years then I forgot you, I put you down,
ingratitude is the necessary curse
of making things new:
I brought my family to see me through,
I brought my homage & my soft remorse,
I brought a book or two

only, including in the end your last
strange poems made under the shadow of death
Your high figures float
again across my mind and all your past
fills my walled garden with your honey breath
wherein I move, a mote.

Behind me twice her necessary knight
she comes like one of Spenser's ladies on
on a white palfrey
and it is cold & full dark in the valley,
though I haven't seen a dragon for days, & faint moonlight
gives my horse footing till dawn.

My lady is all in green, for innocence
I am in black, a terror to my foes
who are numerous & strong.
I haven't lost a battle yet but I am tense
for the first losing. I wipe blood from my nose
and raise up my voice in song.

Hard lies the road behind, hard that ahead
but we are armed & armoured & we trust
entirely one another.
We have beaten down the foulest of them, lust,
and we pace on in peace, like sister & brother,
doing that to which we were bred.

Blow upon blow, his fire-breath hurt me sore,
I upped my broad sword & it hurt him more,
without his talons at a loss
 & dragons are stupid: I wheeled around to the back of him
my charger swift and then I trimmed him
tail-less.

Offering dragons quarter is no good,
they re-grow all their parts & come on again,
they have to be killed.
I set my lance & took him as I would,
in the fiery head, he crumpled like a man,
and one prophecy was fulfilled:

that thrice for Lady Valerie I would suffer
but not be wax from like a base-born duffer,
no no, Sir Henry would win.
until a day that was not prophesied,
having restored her lands. My love & pride
fixed me like a safety-pin.

O land of Connolly & Pearse, what have
ever you done to deserve these tragic masters?
You come & go,
free: nothing happens. Nelson's Pillar blows
but the busses still go there: nothing is changed,
for all these disasters O

We fought our freedom out a long while ago
I can't see that it matters, we can't help you
land of ruined abbeys,
discredited Saints & brainless senators,
roofless castles, enemies of Joyce & Swift,
enemies of Synge,

enemies of Yeats & O'Casey, hold your foul ground
your filthy cousins will come around to you,
barely able to read,
friends of Patrick Kavanagh's & Austin Clarke's
those masters who can both read & write,
in the high Irish style.

Henry in Ireland to Bill underground:
Rest well, who worked so hard, who made a good sound
constantly, for so many years:
your high-jinks delighted the continents & our ears:
you had so many girls your life was a triumph
and you loved your one wife.

At dawn you rose & wrote—the books poured fourth—
you delivered infinite babies, in one great birth—
and your generosity
to juniors made you deeply loved, deeply:
if envy was a Henry trademark, he would envy you,
especially the being through.

Too many journeys lie for him ahead,
too many galleys & page-proofs to be read,
he would like to lie down
in your sweet silence, to whom was not denied
the mysterious late excellence which is the crown
of our trials & our last bride.

325

Control it now, it can't do any good,
your grief for your great friend, killed on the day
he &   his wife &   three
were moving to a larger house across the street.
Our dead frisk us, & later they get better at it,
our wits are stung astray

till all that we can do is groan, bereft:
tears fail: and then we reckon what is left,
not what was lost.
I notice at this point a divided soul,
headed both fore & aft and guess which soul
will swamp & lose:

that hoping forward, brisk & vivid one
of which will nothing ever be heard again.
Advance into the past!
Henry made lists of his surviving friends
& of the vanished on their uncanny errands
and took a deep breath.

Trunks & impedimenta. My manuscript won't go
in my huge Spanish briefcase, some into a bag.
Packing is an India's women's,
I wonder every time how I manage it
& I have done it thirty-four times, by count.
It's time to settle down-O

but not yet. I want to hear the interminable sea
and my spiritual exercises for other civilizations
are well under weigh.
Ships I love, & on ships strangers: Yvette Choinais,
the little man from Cambridge with the little beard
padding about alone barefoot with a little book.

Him Henry never met, but Mlle Choinais
he self-met & swung with on the penultimate day:
O there was a fearful loss,
we could have talked the whole week's journey through
parmi some chaste chat about me & you
and of not being married at twenty-seven the semi-cross

Thrums up from nowhere a distinguisht wail.
the griefs of all his grievous friends, and his,
startling Ballsbridge,
our sedate suburb, the capital of What Is,
a late September fly   goes by, learned & frail,
and Cemetery Ridge

glares down the years of losses to this end
that the note from my bank this morning was stampt with
        Sir Roger Casement,
no 'Sir,' just the portrait & years:
about whom Yeats was so wrong
This distinguisht & sensitive man lived in the grip
of a homosexual obsession, even the 'tools' of native policemen
        excited him.

Yeats knew nothing about life: it was all symbols
 & Wordsworthian egotism: Yeats on Cemetery Ridge
would not have been scared, like you & me,
he would have been, before   the bullet that was his,
studying the movements of the birds,
said disappointed & amazed Henry.

.

337

The mind is incalculable. Greatly excited
to learn from his ex-fiancée, a widow,
that she had remarried
I patted the husband on the shoulder and
abruptly my happy thought became financial:
my god, said Henry to himself,

as they shook hands, that suit cost two hundred dollars!
That lucky fellow, with such a bride & such a down-soft tweed!
Vile envy did not enter his soul
but whisked around the corners all-right. Wow.
Henry missed his chance: he sat down to read
& write, missing the whole

girl or lady & the remarkable tweed.
Shall he put in play again the broad esteem
in which his work was held
agonized? his lonely & his desperate work?
O yes: he would not trade: moments of supreme joy jerk
him on, his other loves quelled & dispelled.

338

According to the Annals of the Four Masters
the West Doorway of the Nuns' Church, Clonmacnoise,
was completed in 1167.
Henry was at that strange point still in Heaven
and so were all his readers. Adrienne & William
slept in possibility,

their wits unwakened, and so did Delmore & Randall
& every reader else upon the earth
or under it.
In a happy proto-silence they or we all waited.
In fact it may be said our breath was bated
waiting for the adventure of sin.

Which took us some one way & some another
like a British traveller in the airport at Bangkok
sweatless among the Orient
reading precisely a dark-blue World's Classics —
I'll bet he loved his father & his mother
which was almost more than Henry could make.

Fan-mail from foreign countries, is that fame?
Imitations & parodies in your own,
translations?
Most of the relevant prizes, your private name
splashed on page one, with a photograph alone
or you with your lovely wife?

Interviews on television & radio
on various continents, can that be fame?
Henry could not find out.
Before he left the ship at Cobh he was photographed,
I don't know how they knew he was coming
He said as little as possible.

They wanted to know whether   his sources of inspiration
might now be Irish: I cried out 'of course'
 & waved him off with my fountain pen.
The tender left the liner & headed for shore.
Cobh (pronounced Khove) approached, our luggage was ready,
and anonymously we went into Customs.

A lone letter from a young man: that is fame.

Henry's pride in his house was almost fierce,
Henry, who took no pride in anything
only but work hard done:
an angry ghost appeared & leaned for years
on his front stoop; elderly Henry spread his wings
one by one by one

until the traffic could not see it more:
he's leaving for America & things,
things.
Deep in concussion, deep in extra love,
he sorted out his extra fate. He sings
& clowns

and is wiser than the next man, in so many towns
across a continent. We must be careful of it,
the special gift,
the wardrobes wide & wider. Pained eyes, Henry's.
Unmanly slovenly love took him at times
and passed him back.

They came ashore with erections
 & laid the Irish maidens in large numbers
then in 1588.
Spaniards are vile & virile.
History after all is a matter of fumbles.
Man's derelictions, man's fate,

is a matter of sorry record. Somehow the prizes
come at the wrong times to the proper people
 & vice versa.
The great ships, confused in tempest,
drove on the shoals. Accepting ladies
crowded the northern shore.

In they plunged, in half-armour, with their strength
returned to the personal. Philip's on his own.
These fragrant maidens
are good to a man out of the sea, at length,
in a new world, and each new man, alone,
made up his own destiny.

Chilled in this Irish pub I wish my loves
well, well to strangers, well to all his friends,
seven or so in number,
I forgive my enemies, especially two,
races his heart, at so much magnanimity,
can it at all be true?

—Mr Bones, you on a trip outside yourself.
Has you seen a medicine man? You sound will-like,
a testament & such.
Is you going?—Oh, I suffer from a strike
& a strike & three balls: I stand up for much,
Wordsworth & that sort of thing.

The pitcher dreamed. He threw a hazy curve,
I took it in my stride & out I struck,
lonesome Henry.
These Songs are not meant to be understood, you understand.
They are only meant to terrify & comfort.
Lilac was found in his hand.

In sight of a more peaceful country, just beyond,
 & just in sight—ilex & magnolia, land
rimmed by a bountiful sea—
Henry took stock of where he now might be
in his own warring state. He stood perplexed
as to where to go next,

forward or backward: he could not stay still,
the decision came: his rotors floated well
to take him back or ahead.
Here he paused, though, & thought of those whom he was leaving
 & those whom he would be missing without grieving
in the fair of the land ahead.

'My friends are full' he muttered to himself,
'I'll make no more, so many now are dead.
Backward is the gallant word,
and grapple to my heart the splendid rest,
to leave the new land unknown & undistressed'—
The happy rotors whirred.

Henry saw with Tolstoyan clarity
his muffled purpose. He described the folds—
not a symbol in the place.
Naked the man came forth in his mask, to be.
Illnesses from encephalitis to colds
shook his depths & his surface.

When he dressed up & up, his costumes varied
with the southeast wind, but he remained aware.
Awareness was most of what he had.
The terrible chagrin to which he was married—
derelict Henry's siege mentality—
stability, I will stay

in my monastery until my death
& the fate my actions have so hardly earned.
The horizon is all cloud.
Leaves on leaves on leaves of books I've turned
and I know nothing, Henry said aloud,
with his ultimate breath.

Sluggish, depressed, & with no mail to cheer,
he lies in Ireland's rains bogged down, aware
of definite mental pain.
He hasn't a friend for a thousand miles to the west
and only two in London, he counted & guessed:
ladies he might see again.

He has an interview to give in London
but the ladies have never married, frolicsomes
as long ago they were,
must he impute to him their spinsterhood
& further groan, as for the ones he stood
up & married fair?

Connection with Henry seemed to be an acre in Hell,
he crossed himself with horror. Doubtless a bell
ought to've been hung on Henry
to warn a-many lovely ladies off
before they had too much, which was enough,
and set their calves to flee.

.

.

O yes I wish her well. Let her come on
to Henry's regions, with her mortal wound.
In so far as repair
is possible, we'll lie her in the sun
forever, with to protect her a great hound,
so that she lies in peace there.

Until her lover comes: let him be good
quietly to her, and her blocked faith restore
in the mountains & the roar
of the grand sea of tumbling pebbles: could
anyone anywhere ask more?
Her patience is exemplary.

Cold & golden lay the high heroine
in a wilderness of bears. Let one man in.
One is enough.
Fish for the master, who will do you well,
rely not on the stormy citadel—
it's a matter of love.

To the edge of Europe, the eighteenth edge,
the ancient edge, Henry sailed full of thought
and rich with high-wrought designs,
for a tranquil mind & to fulfil a pledge
he gave himself to end a labour, sought
but now his mind not finds

conformable itself to that forever
or any more of the stretch of Henry's years.
Strange & new outlines
blur the old project. Soon they dissever
the pen & the heart, the old heart with its fears
& the daughter for which it pines.

Fresh toils the lightning over the Liffey, wild
and the avenues, like Paris's, are rain
and Henry is here for a while
of many months, along with the squalls of a child,
thirty years later. I will not come again
or not come with this style.

Wordsworth, thou form almost divine, cried Henry,
'the egotistical sublime' said Keats,
oh ho, you lovely man!
make from the rafters some mere sign to me
whether when after this raving heart which beats
& which to beat began

Long so years since   stops   I may (ah) expect
a fresh version of living or if I stop
wholly.
Oblongs attend my convalescence, wreckt
and now again, by many full propt up,
not irreversible Henry.

Punctured Henry wondered would he die
forever, all his fine body forever lost
and his very useful mind?
Hopeless & violent the man will lie,
on decades' questing, whose crazed hopes have crossed
to wind up here blind.

At Henry's bier let some thing fall out well:
enter there none who somewhat has to sell,
the music ancient & gradual,
the voices solemn but the grief subdued,
no hairy jokes but everybody's mood
subdued, subdued,

until the Dancer comes, in a short short dress
hair black & long & loose, dark dark glasses,
uptilted face,
pallor & strangeness, the music changes
to 'Give!' & 'Ow!' and how! the music changes,
she kicks a backward limb

on tiptoe, pirouettes, & she is free
to the knocking music, sails, dips, & suddenly
returns to the terrible gay
occasion hopeless & mad, she weaves, it's hell,
she flings to her head a leg, bobs, all is well,
she dances Henry away.

The marker slants, flowerless, day's almost done,
I stand above my father's grave with rage,
often, often before
I've made this awful pilgrimage to one
who cannot visit me, who tore his page
out: I come back for more,

I spit upon this dreadful banker's grave
who shot his heart out in a Florida dawn
O ho alas alas
When will indifference come, I moan & rave
I'd like to scrabble till I got right down
away down under the grass

and ax the casket open ha to see
just how he's taking it, which he sought so hard
we'll tear apart
the mouldering grave clothes ha & then Henry
will heft the ax once more, his final card,
and fell it on the start.

385

My daughter's heavier. Light leaves are flying.
Everywhere in enormous numbers turkeys will be dying
and other birds, all their wings.
They never greatly flew. Did they wish to?
I should know. Off away somewhere once I knew
such things.

Or good Ralph Hodgson back then did, or does.
The man is dead whom Eliot praised. My praise
follows and flows too late.
Fall is grievy, brisk. Tears behind the eyes
almost fall. Fall comes to us as a prize
to rouse us toward our fate.

My house is made of wood and it's made well,
unlike us. My house is older than Henry;
that's fairly old.
If there were a middle   ground between things and the soul
or if the sky resembled more the sea,
I wouldn't have to scold

                                        my heavy daughter.

INDEX OF FIRST LINES